Feminism for the World

Feminism for the World

Lola Olufemi, Françoise Vergès, Silvia Federici,
Verónica Gago, Zahra Ali, Rama Salla Dieng,
Sayak Valencia and Djamila Ribeiro

Translated from French and Spanish by Fionn Petch
and from Portuguese by Sophie Lewis

First published as *Gagner le monde* by La Fabrique éditions, 2023

English edition first published 2025 by Pluto Press
New Wing, Somerset House, Strand, London WC2R 1LA
and Pluto Press, Inc.
1930 Village Center Circle, 3-834, Las Vegas, NV 89134

www.plutobooks.com

Copyright © La Fabrique éditions, 2023, 2025

English language translations of 'On the Feminist Movement's Desire for Theory', 'The Collection "Femmes en luttes de tous les pays"', 'Truly Radical', 'Intifada (انتفاضة) and the Feminist Imagination', and 'Of Course the Word is a Weapon' Copyright © Fionn Petch 2025

English language translation of 'Motherhood from a Iabá Point of View' Copyright © Sophie Lewis 2025

The right of Lola Olufemi, Françoise Vergès, Silvia Federici, Verónica Gago, Zahra Ali, Rama Salla Dieng, Sayak Valencia and Djamila Ribeiro to be identified as the authors of this work has been asserted in accordance with the Copyright, Designs and Patents Act 1988.

British Library Cataloguing in Publication Data
A catalogue record for this book is available from the British Library

ISBN   978 0 7453 5033 2   Paperback
ISBN   978 0 7453 5035 6   PDF
ISBN   978 0 7453 5034 9   EPUB

This book is printed on paper suitable for recycling and made from fully managed and sustained forest sources. Logging, pulping and manufacturing processes are expected to conform to the environmental standards of the country of origin.

Typeset by Stanford DTP Services, Northampton, England

Simultaneously printed in the United Kingdom and United States of America

EU GPSR Authorised Representative
LOGOS EUROPE, 9 rue Nicolas Poussin, 17000, LA ROCHELLE, France
Email: Contact@logoseurope.eu

Contents

Introduction   vi

1. On the Feminist Movement's Desire for Theory   1
   Verónica Gago

2. The Collection 'Femmes en luttes de tous les pays'   21
   Françoise Vergès

3. Motherhood from a Iabá Point of View   40
   Djamila Ribeiro

4. Communism's Promise   57
   Lola Olufemi

5. Truly Radical   87
   Sayak Valencia

6. Intifada (انتفاضة) and the Feminist Imagination   114
   Zahra Ali

7. 'Of Course the Word is a Weapon'   134
   Rama Salla Dieng

8. For Maria Mies   155
   Silvia Federici

Introduction

The problem of transmission is one that inevitably arises for all militant traditions. What are the paths by which we inherit past struggles, whether victorious or defeated, together with the collective intelligence that was deployed through them? How to work with this inexhaustible heritage in the present? Such questions are all the more acute for the most combative branches of feminism, which for a long time have had to push back against attempts by the state to co-opt them, and more recently the commercial or reactionary appropriation of their themes and slogans. Eight years after #MeToo, at a time when a feminist aspiration for justice and equality has taken hold of a generation and is firing on all cylinders, the texts gathered here speak to us of the present moment through the detour of history.

The history of feminism is often presented as a succession of 'waves' that encompass specific currents of thought and organisations, each of which sought to rectify the impasses reached by the preceding ones. With its focus on Western Europe and North America, this approach tends to overlook feminist experiences in Africa, Latin America, the former Soviet Union, Asia, the Middle East or the Caribbean that do not fit neatly into the categories and periods it proposes. Nor is this its only flaw: it also relies on a linear vision of events that papers over setbacks and does little to guard against the old trick of time that feminists know all too well: the backlash.

In her book *The Commune Form: The Transformation of Everyday Life* (2024),[1] Kristin Ross shows how the struggles of peasant farmers to defend their lands in the 1960s–1970s,

INTRODUCTION

thought to have been confined to the period, are taking on new meaning in light of current battles against the disappearance of natural spaces and the appropriation of public resources. Around the world, contemporary activism against sexist violence, the exploitation of reproductive labour brought to light by the COVID-19 pandemic, and the fascist policies that target women and the most vulnerable sections of the population, are making some of the struggles that seemed to belong to the past topical again. The ambition of this collection of essays is to re-examine them, not as an archive but as a living source of inspiration, as moments that defined our present. To cultivate, as Verónica Gago writes in Chapter 1, 'the capacity to return to a "grand" epoch due to a collective capacity to raise problems, probe them and open them up in a manner that does not necessarily imply resolving them directly'.

The authors of these texts all share one thing in common: they write from, or in dialogue with, the feminisms and the struggles of the Global South. What emerges is a method for thinking about and practising the paths of international solidarity, attentive to the local contexts and to the specific experiences of women, from which it becomes possible to build a common language and offer a 'vision of the future speaking not only to women but also to the broader struggle for human liberation and the regeneration of nature', in the words of Silvia Federici. Over the course of these pages, we witness the astonishing ability of feminist concepts and slogans – and of the activists themselves – to traverse the frontiers between decades and continents, which is what gives feminism its power, and its ability to change the world.

Notes

1. Kristin Ross, *The Commune Form: The Transformation of Everyday Life* (London: Verso, 2024).

1

On the Feminist Movement's Desire for Theory

Verónica Gago

A brief overview

The cycle of feminist mobilisations and organisations that emerged internationally in 2016 consolidated in the years 2017, 2018 and 2019. The strikes in Poland and Argentina staged in 2016 were connected to newly launched movements, such as Ni Una Menos ('Not one woman less') in Argentina in 2015, and gathered momentum from them. I would argue that with the strike as a tool, their political character changed, passing an organisational threshold. By 2017, International Women's Day on 8 March had become a global day of feminist strike, with different forms of organisation in dozens of countries.

In those three years from 2017 to 2019, the movement grew in strength thanks to four factors: 1) the feminist 8 March strike became established; 2) the international character of the movement expanded, clearly driven by the Global South; 3) the link up with abortion rights campaigns, also international in character; and 4) the feminist movement converged with working-class and indigenous dynamics of protest in several Latin American countries.

During these three years, we witnessed what I interpret as an unprecedented combination for the feminist movement: the conjunction of mass scale and radicalness.[1] Therein lies the singularity of what we might characterise as a cycle, which I understand as the emergence of a 'moment' of widespread uprising. In this sense, I am interested in identifying a set of dynamics that helps to explain this singularity, making it intelligible without simply ascribing it to the notion of 'causes'. I will summarise these briefly, while noting that they do not constitute a single schema.

First, the movement arrives at a reading of the violences that, starting with the body and the territories it inhabits, expands their connection to make sense of institutional, economic, racist and sexist violences. This way of bringing about a *systemic* reading of violences shifts the axis of interpersonal violences, and relocates it in a structural key that nevertheless remains situated. For this same reason, since it starts out from experience and does not limit itself to a question of the individual, it achieves a practical understanding of the violences of capital in its neoliberal phase. The everyday is not synonymous with smallness, but rather reactivates a critique that deepens the understanding of this moment of capitalist depredation we are living through. I will return to this later.

Second, this enables a politics of transversality in terms of *alliances*, not only of the construction of *issues* and *demands*, but also in the very definition of social conflict. In concrete terms, I am referring to producing a feminist politics for all spaces and broadening feminist intervention to issues that were not necessarily directly associated with their concerns and areas of involvement: from pensions to land ownership, from water pollution to school curricula. It is not a sum or aggregation of demands, but an elaboration of how each of these areas can be reconsidered from a feminist perspective and in what sense they are spaces of engagement towards which the movement expands. Nor is this limited to a theoretical analysis of an intersectional kind, but rather it extends

On the Feminist Movement's Desire for Theory

to a political combination of struggles and the embedding of feminism in existing organisations working on these issues.

Third, the feminist movement generates politics at both international and local levels, while connecting the politics of masses on the streets with the changes in everyday social relations. These are two closely related questions of scale. This is a key point for considering a revolutionary process in terms of the mutations of connections, capable of affecting the forms of organising the work, suited to building subjective capacities to imagine other ways of life and at the same time encouraging direct intervention in the specific circumstances of each place. The feminist movement knots together micropolitics and macropolitics because experience interlaces geographies that make of bodies and territories planes on which to observe the effects of the local and international, circumstantial, national and global. In this recent cycle of mobilisations, internationalism – or what we also call the cross-border make-up of the movement – is experienced as a favourable terrain for its expansion, operating almost like an irrigation system that opens up new space for itself.

The pandemic as a handbrake to the feminist revolution

The pandemic that began in 2020 and continued well into 2021 interrupted this expanding cycle of feminist mobilisations and struggle. We cannot help but be struck by the kind of retreat it imposed, as it seems to have formed an exact counter-image of what the movement was able to forcefully expose and break down, such as relations of obedience, oppression and exploitation.

The urgent need for social reproduction unleashed by the COVID-19 crisis translated into confinement to family and domestic spaces. This confinement imposed a tendency towards the 'undoing' of all disobedience in relation to the questioning of the home as a safe space, understood in its heteropatriarchal framework. Such a withdrawal into the spaces of proximity also had a class-based segmentation effect on the city, preventing diagonal, transversal displacements, which were key to the boiling up of transfeminist alliances.

The imposition of gender mandates with the urgency of the crisis aimed to shut down the temporality of another crisis: the one opened by the disregard of these mandates of care tied to binary gender roles. But, in addition, the feminist strike as a tool for the rejection of unpaid work returned as an intensification of these tasks. Under the term 'essential work', this has put the spotlight back on the work done by women, lesbians, travestis and transsexuals, subsistence farmers and immigrants, whose productive capacity has historically been scorned and who have not been recognised as workers. The term 'essential' was used as a cover for endless working days, unlimited availability in the face of emergencies, the invention of expedients in the face of scarcity, and the use of accumulated knowledge to cope with daily deprivation. We have seen a historical manipulation applied on a massive scale to these tasks and to a huge number of jobs linked to social reproduction – from education to health, including all forms of care work, agro-ecological production and helplines – that consisted of naturalising the work of reproduction, but this time in the open, and no longer just within the closed confines of the home. At the same time, reproductive tasks and new forms of care were being 'returned' to the home in the form of rapidly expanding remote working. The twist, however, is more complicated. We talk about work, but it appears that it ceases to be work as soon as it is described as 'essential'. It is recognised as having a value, but that value seems to be fundamentally symbolic and related to its urgency. The same tasks were publicly claimed in the pandemic in symbolic but unpaid terms, denying another fundamental element of the strike:

ON THE FEMINIST MOVEMENT'S DESIRE FOR THEORY

the problematisation of reproductive work as a synonym for unpaid work.

The novel character of the pandemic, then, has been experienced in relation to a set of questions – sensible, emotional, political and conceptual – that the feminist movement in recent years had succeeded in framing and highlighting. By this I mean that the framework for understanding this exceptional event would not have been the same without the prior existence of the struggles we referred to above. In particular, it calls into question the concrete territory of the exploitation of paid and unpaid work, and the contemporary forms of privatisation of social reproduction. Both questions have acquired a singular relevance in the context of the mobilisations and strikes.

Then, there is a second movement. If the pandemic functioned as a laboratory for the patriarchal and familial reconfiguration of ties, the feminist movement has opposed it with the construction of support networks, infrastructures of collective provision, and a commitment to the de-domestication of care. Among these practices, we may point to what Judith Butler calls the ethical question of interdependence in the pandemic: 'What makes a life liveable is a question that implicitly shows us that the life we live is never exclusively our own, that the conditions for a liveable life have to be secured, and not just for me but for lives and living processes more generally.' This, she argues, is impeded if the notion of 'private property that describes my body or presumes my individuality is accepted as methodology'.[2]

As I mentioned at the beginning, this cycle has succeeded, with its mass scale, in making feminist practices a way of extending the contours of a body that is linked to the territory, inventing a language that speaks of body-territories in order to think about the connection between ecological crisis and the possibility of other non-proprietary sovereignties (I am thinking of 'food sovereignty', for example, a historical demand of campesino movements).

The feminist challenge to the model of possessive individualism as a way of understanding the world has had enormous power in the experiences of organisation, mobilisation and subversion of everyday life. To rethink care and protection, for example, by saying *'no me cuida la policía, me cuidan mis amigas'* ('the police don't look after me, my female friends look after me'); to understand this expansion of the sensibility of the body by declaring *'si tocan a una, respondemos todes'* ('if they touch one of us, we all respond'); or by making it clear that *'no vamos a pagar la crisis con nuestros cuerpos y territorios'* ('we are not going to pay for the crisis with our bodies and territories'). These are all examples in which, in a simple and powerful way, this collective experience discloses and empowers itself.

During the pandemic, this framework was maintained as a key to understanding what was happening. This is what made it possible to denounce domestic violence in conditions of forced confinement, but also the violence of eviction, placing housing at the centre of the conflict. From the Ni Una Menos collective, in partnership with the tenants' union, we launched the campaign *'La casa no puede ser lugar de violencias machistas ni de especulación inmobiliaria'* ('The home is no place for macho violence or real estate speculation'), involving ourselves in a way that makes visible the denunciations of violence that grew in the moment of 'confinement' but also the ways in which confinement was made to coexist with the threat of eviction. The counter-methodology – as opposed to the methodology of private property Butler speaks of – was a sustained practice of transfeminist networks during the pandemic, capable of forming a collective body just when the paradigm of security was a call to isolate.

On the Feminist Movement's Desire for Theory

From this starting point, we were able to rethink the home as a place where new enclosures were being practised: spaces of financial recolonisation for capital, where debts have continued to accumulate due to the global rise in energy, food and housing prices. In a recent paper, Luci Cavallero and I identified four intertwining dynamics that were introduced to Argentine households during the pandemic: 1) Rising household debt for the purchase of basic goods, a consequence of income restrictions but also of the emergence of *new* debts (for utilities and emergencies). 2) Rising debt for rent (both for rent owed and debt for inability to pay rent) and increasing exposure to eviction as a result of accumulating debt. All this is combined with the intensification of property speculation (on both the formal and informal markets) through the rise (via dollarisation) in rents and the restriction of supply as a result of new regulations. 3) The reorganisation and intensification of reproductive (especially unpaid) and productive working days in the same space. 4) The intrusion of financial technology (FinTech) into the home, through mobile payments, e-ticketing and online banking.[3]

The pandemic, without question, attempted a re-privatisation manoeuvre, a kind of 'call to order' to the occupation of the streets by feminisms and the reorganisation of the domestic sphere. In fact, the transformation of homes into 'home-workshops' (a term we can reclaim from the 1970s, now without its association of Fordist factories) continue to be subject to extraordinary conditions, even after the COVID-19 emergency.

This continuum is a nerve centre for thinking about the present moment. The 'end' of the pandemic is in fact part of a new scenario of impoverishment in which Latin America is breaking records.[4]

Simultaneously, over the two years of the pandemic, the acceleration of the extractivist dynamic saw new momentum in terms of monopolistic concentration and brutality, continued by means of war and its geopolitical agenda. In our region, the extractivist advance reorganises the territory to the point of fragmenting it into militarised zones divvied up between private corporations.

We can also speak of a war that is now unfolding in the sphere of social reproduction, like the one that prolongs what appeared to be exceptional conditions during the pandemic, remaining in place well beyond it.

We are experiencing an intensification in the concrete, material conditions of impoverishment with which the possibility of collective organisation must contend. Popular and feminist organisations are obliged to find immediate solutions, to remain in a 'state of emergency'. In this way they are, once again, *confined* to the most pressing social support efforts. The margins of time and energy for creative overflow diminish to the extent that meeting basic needs takes more and more effort.

The channelling of this unease at the 'disorder' of a daily life that has shed all its security, of a social reproduction that is *under attack*, finds an eloquent outlet of expression and emotional understanding in right-wing discourse. If the feminist movement decisively revealed the ground-level effects of neoliberal violence and identified the type of social relation that makes it possible, the response to this feminist challenge raises the stakes but builds on these same challenges. To this end, the pandemic has been the great dress rehearsal. It brought about a nuclear family-based, property-owning and racist withdrawal that contests what feminists have described as the problem of interdependence. In this way, we are invited to base our dependence on others on racist models of distribution (who deserves care and who doesn't), according to a property-owning meritocracy (who holds property titles as a guarantee of their rights), and according to a moral and biological vision of relationships (where the heteropatriarchal family is reinstituted as the norm).

The feminist movement inhabited by a desire for theory

It is possible to observe, from the outset of this cycle of struggles, another notable feature of the feminist movement: it is inhabited by a desire for theory. By this I mean a vital, organic need to generate concepts, to find words, to rehearse different ways of narrating what is happening. This trait differentiates the feminist movement from other social movements, where the anti-intellectual gesture is often trotted out as a kind of guarantee of authentic experience.

We need only point to the proliferation of slogans, songs, fanzines, reading groups, books and journals. There is a vast quantity of debates, meetings, seminars, self-education spaces, new university programmes, etc. This theoretical and political explosion brings with it a specific challenge: how to stop *cry* and *concept* from becoming completely separate. How to prevent the chant '*¡ya basta, paren de matarnos!*' ('no more, stop killing us!') – which lies at the root of movements like Ni Una Menos – from remaining just a cry of pain, and ensures that it is deployed in the struggle, which includes terms both conceptual and programmatic. It is not a question of an opposition between a non-conceptual cry and a developed theory, but rather of a different kind of displacement: this 'no more!' opens up a field of crucial theoretical, narrative and argumentative debate.

The anti-intellectual prejudice holds considerable sway among intellectuals and militants and has become embedded in a series of commonplaces that continue to operate; for example, the hackneyed division between thinking and doing; between producing and experiencing; and between comfort and risk. These are undoubtedly the extremes that produce caricatures: militant self-sacrifice in the name of practice, as if it were devoid of ideas; and the intellectual's limpid adoration of the heaven of concepts, as if they were pure abstractions. Despite such stereotypes, they continue to define the boundaries of a map that has nevertheless undergone considerable change. I believe that in this cycle of mass, radical feminist mobilisations a change has come about in this sensible, conceptual and political distribution. The question of anti-intellectual prejudice can also be reversed: every time this binary re-emerges (in its crudest formulation: those who think and those who act), we can identify a disciplinary response to a shift in the relationship between thought and praxis. That is why anti-intellectualism, rather than being a nod to popular feeling and the wealth of experience (as often dramatised), is in fact a call to order and a reaffirmation of classist, sexist and racist hierarchies.

In 1906, Rosa Luxemburg described as 'grand' an epoch that 'raises masses of problems, *enormous* problems'; as a moment 'that provokes [...] and stimulates "criticism, irony and deeper significance" and stirs up passions'.[5] When I refer to the desire for theory of the feminist movement, I mean the capacity to return to a 'grand' epoch which has a collective capacity to raise problems, probe them and open them up in a manner that does not necessarily imply resolving them directly. Yet, it generates the experience of formulating them, of being a part of their redefinition, to the point of experiencing the limits of what can be thought, while avoiding the shortcuts of other methods that appear to bring a greater sense of resolution. In this way, we can reposition a capacity for 'reflective indocility', to use Foucault's term, as a diffuse sensibility that connects conceptualisation with disobedience.

Further, this desire for theory is connected with the very dynamic of inventing names and narratives for what is necessary to say in another way. Without a doubt, this versatility

On the Feminist Movement's Desire for Theory

of conceptual language expresses a capacity to make a praxis of a mode of questioning, with its steps and counter-steps, its rehearsals and its wagers. It is no coincidence, as bell hooks said, that 'the feminist willingness to change direction when necessary has been a major source of strength and vitality in feminist struggle', as well as at other historical moments.[6] The familiarity with this ability to start speaking a new language, self-criticise and reopen past debates is connected with the vitality of a movement that thinks on its feet. This is what thought is: an attribute of movement. bell hooks adds that 'our theory must remain fluid, open, receptive to new information' in order to stay in touch with everything that changes in our lives.[7] This fluidity imbues the movement with theoretical depth. Yet, I want to add that the cycle we are discussing, this conceptualisation, is something that receives strong momentum from the Global South.

And here, I think another point is worth emphasising: the readiness of the movement to generate its own voices in which to dialogue and exchange, putting under tension the other classic geopolitical distribution between those who take action but when it comes to narratives appear struck dumb or speak *solely* using pre-existing grammars. The decolonising dimension of theoretical practice – as Bolivian-Aymara anarchist theorist Silvia Rivera Cusicanqui has long argued – is a challenge taken on by the feminist movement, which forges theory out of struggle, which refuses to disassociate mobilisation from concept and which appropriates texts and invents terminology in order to make them converse with the situations and circumstances we face.

This work is also one of territorialising concepts. As Maria Mies proposes, we can treat concepts as if they were territories.[8] This implies that concepts can be 'occupied'. I associate the desire for theory with the ways in which the feminist movement takes charge of *liberating* certain concepts. There is a battle being waged in the terrain of language and pedagogies that involves the movement's determination to produce collective texts. Texts that can be passed back and forth between the streets and the home, and from the home to the streets, shaping an anti-patriarchal grammar that makes light of the frontiers between these spaces.

This is why I would argue that the desire for theory drives a capacity for enunciation and action on the part of feminist struggles, one that involves the challenge of decolonising theoretical practice. I return to the three points I set out at the beginning as new elements in this cycle, where the entanglement between massiveness and radicalness entails a desire for theory. On the one hand, this is expressed in the need to reopen the collective debate around violence and its different forms, which presupposes both rejecting the language of crimes of passion and of interpersonal violence to establish femicides as political events. It also implies removing domestic violence from the private sphere. Yet even more, I would argue, it begins to systematise a 'theory of violence' in which concepts take their power from the streets. Without doubt, this offers multiple potential roadmaps.

I'm particularly interested in how the notion of war has been returned to the centre of analysis by the feminist perspective, systemically establishing a characterisation of contemporary violence. This analysis, especially with regard to femicidal violence – seen as an individualisation of war – has two fundamental characteristics: 1) it shifts the notion of war to a different grammar of conflict; and 2) it renews the need for a theory of a violence without being *demotivating* or *victimising*. By this I refer to the way in which recent feminist struggles have generated a site from which contemporary neoliberal violence can be described without abandoning the deployment of a capacity for political action. This mode of interweaving a conceptualisation of violence with forms of action on the streets, in neighbourhoods and in social organisations indicates the importance of the theoretical territory.

I believe that a number of feminist formulations, based on the conceptualisation of a war on women, provide a framework for understanding the new type of wars, while also enabling readings of other wars. Repositioning the term 'war' to speak of the 'state of permanent war' against certain bodies and certain territories has helped to popularise the thesis of Silvia Federici regarding the extent to which the devaluation of the life and reproductive work of women, migrants and campesinos driven by this phase of contemporary globalisation shapes a neoliberal violence that has not been subsumed into mechanisms of subjective pacification, and not understood solely in terms of surveillance societies.[9] The 'new forms of war' capable of analysing violence against the bodies of women and dissident bodies in relation to the economies of illegal capital – as Rita Segato argues – likewise refresh the lexicon with strategic examination of a war that is no longer between two clearly identifiable sides on a single field of battle. For her part, Raquel Gutiérrez Aguilar has characterised it in terms of the systematic aggression pursued against the fabrics of community and communal reproduction, and their direct connection to the cruelty of attacks on women and nature. In this regard, the way in which anti-extractivist struggles are seen as a war of territorial conquest, displacement of populations, and assassination of resistance leaders, also brings out multiple concrete examples of this narrative that sharpens the perspective of war (see the work of Mina Navarro, among others).

By this I wish to emphasise how neoliberal violences as elements for thinking about war have been placed on the table by a set of feminist debates that are both *accommodated* and *amplified* in mass movements. This same mobilisation has succeeded in establishing that gender-based violence is a structural part of an ongoing war, and an updating of the variations that have occurred in the very dynamics of what we understand war to mean. Where the experience of seeking our own narrative liberates the power to act, we see the desire for theory as praxis become effective.

The alliances that make a movement

At the start of this text, I mentioned a second element of the feminist movement: the capacity to build alliances as a political practice capable of expanding the definition and intelligibility of conflicts. Alliances do not follow a logic of consensus but of strategy. They are built on the basis of a shared objective. In this sense, they are experiments connected to political circumstances. They operate in that timeframe. However, experimenting with alliances, testing their efficacy, vividly feeling the expansion of possibilities that they unfold, makes them a desirable resource. In other words, they are often sought after because of the memory of what they enable, and this is the first step towards their materialisation.

Political alliances, unlike the formulas of pseudo-solidarity, are organised around a shared problem, cultivating proximity between different struggles through consensual evaluation of priorities. As such, they are a political technology that serves to determine: 1) what is most urgent; 2) what the plans for intervention are; and 3) the route map for the conflict.

Alliances are what enable conflicts to be escalated: to project them more widely, expand their scale, make them audible to more people, and even to achieve what may be considered a victory. Alliances conceive a formation that doesn't disregard particular interests – and in this sense they mobilise a pragmatic intelligence – but also establish a shared plane ready to take in other possible meanings of belonging, commitment and affiliation.

Those alliances that bypass the predictable paths of a conflict are the first thing at risk, whether due to forms of financing that segment us, to the dynamics of setting a specific 'agenda', or to electoral calculations.

Alliances are concrete forms of thinking beyond the individual or, rather, of facing up to the dependency of individuals with regard to their alliances. An alliance with the environment triggers an anti-extractivist perspective. An alliance among neighbours allows us to think of how to de-financialise housing. An alliance between students and women workers in the informal sector makes it possible to establish a community school. An alliance formed in a trans and non-binary assembly secures the liberation of a lesbian imprisoned for defending her rights. An alliance enables directors of public hospitals and independent abortion providers to effectively implement a law. Without these alliances (all of which refer to concrete situations for the feminist movement in Argentina), such achievements would not be realised.

In this regard, alliances are preceded by conflicts. Alliances emerge as confrontation and not as an a priori calculation of sectors working together. This is also why the definition of the conflict depends on the alliance: the way the conflict is defined and described is part of how this conflict is understood in terms of the actors involved. Therefore, in order to build alliances, we need to share a conflict, and being involved in a conflict means being aware of how this conflict affects us.

Weaving transfeminist alliances entails a political action of producing proximity to a conflict from a perspective of different subjects and collectives. In which instances are these alliances forged? How can these types of alliances be developed? The answer is hard work, that is, political work. A great deal of time is spent organising meetings, assemblies, initiatives, working hard together to generate a shared definition. The work of alliances generates a collective intelligence that is able to express itself in slogans; therein lies their polyphonic authorship.

Here, I also wish to associate this practice of transversal construction to an effect of theoretical production, in two senses: as a reading of the situation and as a form of synthesis in political slogans.

Slogans as collective intelligence

I have already observed how alliances make movements. This is a mode of understanding the concrete formation of a mass scale that is neither spontaneous nor rests solely on established relations of belonging. As I underlined above, their vectors of radicality are reactivated to the extent that their capacity to incorporate conflict increases. I then added the possibility of detecting in them a desire for theory, capable of making the theoretical terrain a strategic and non-delegable space. To conclude, I would like to dwell on the slogans that *make movement*, to take up the beautiful formulation of Julieta Kirkwood, who made feminist theory by considering that a movement is made up of questions.[10] Thinking in terms of questions that *make* movement means adopting a process of analysis that establishes the critical and interrogative dimension as a force.

From questions to slogans there is a *strategic* formulation. Not because the questions are lacking in it. Rather, on the contrary: the interrogative form is strategic because it opens up a horizon. 'What does the feminist movement want? Demands and reasons' was the title of a pamphlet by the 8M Feminist Commission in Madrid in 2019. But I want to point out that slogans are theoretical-political approaches to spread the conceptual findings of a movement.

As we have known since Lenin, slogans have a validity in time and space: their power comes from how they connect

ON THE FEMINIST MOVEMENT'S DESIRE FOR THEORY

bodies and proclamations that express a particular circumstance. Each slogan, he claimed, 'must be deduced from the totality of specific features of a definite political situation'.[11] When we read slogans that acquire meaning beyond borders, they convey *dates* (in which these words express a moment) and *theses* that organise a way of understanding, and indeed of directing, what is occurring. Rosa Luxemburg was even more optimistic in this regard, arguing that whoever gave the slogan determined the direction of the struggle.

Slogans express, without a doubt, transformations of both bodies and of atmosphere, which are translated into forms of living violence, self-defence, insecurity, collective strength, and the struggle for everything that makes up the determination to live in ever more critical contexts. These slogans imply transformations in bodies, materialise thresholds in relations, establish a collective horizon, articulate a language, sum up a whole epoch.

The proliferation of recent feminist slogans, the movement's ability to translate them and shift them to new geographies, while reaffirming them as its own, can be read as a shared text and programme.

At the same time, slogans demonstrate a certain experience of *intranslatability*: they are strongly connected to the explosion of their sound, their rhythm, and often to poetic or historical meanings that are hard to preserve in another language. That said, they are also increasingly becoming a part of shared language, and indeed in a manner that exercises differences and marks ruptures: what is the dissonance between '#NiUnaMenos' and '#MeToo'? Is the song about *poder popular* – 'popular power' – understood everywhere as a feminist demand? How has the slogan *No es amor, es trabajo no pago* – 'It's not love. It's unpaid work' – spread so far, having leapt from a text by Silvia Federici to the streets, or the graffiti *¡Ni la tierra ni las mujeres son territorios de conquista!*

FEMINISM FOR THE WORLD

– 'Neither land nor women are territories for conquest!' – by the Mujeres Creando collective, which has become a collective anti-extractivist motto?

There is a historical process of migration. The slogan originating in Mexico *Vivas nos queremos* – 'we want/love ourselves alive' – echoes that of the Mothers of the Plaza de Mayo when in the midst of the Argentine dictatorship they chanted '*vivos se los llevaron, vivos los queremos*' ('they were taken alive, we want them alive') to demand the return of their disappeared children. Just like the phrase *Ni una menos* – 'not one woman less' – was taken from Mexican poet Susana Chávez and became a cross-border movement, repositioning Ciudad Juárez in its proximity. A whole cartography could be mapped of the re-emergences, reinterpretations, appearances and translations as quests for new meaning. We might say that slogans achieve what Josefina Ludmer attributed to speculation: to give a syntax to the ideas of others from a territory in which we use them. This means that translating slogans, just like speculating, is a material practice of use that puts into play a conflict between appropriation and invention and presupposes modes of rec-reation capable of grappling between the self and the other, between the immaterial and the territorial, between diverse temporalities. The translation of slogans allows for this mode of speculation as a collective, but always situated, variation.

It is no coincidence that in this cycle of feminist mobilisation a phenomenon has arisen like that of the Chilean collective LasTesis, whose very name is an endorsement of theoretical theses led out onto the street by the hand of text and performance.[12] The song '*Un violador en tu camino*' ('The rapist is you') went viral around the globe because it so eloquently summed up the state of debate of the movement, formulas taken from feminist theory that have become a part of the collective consciousness because they pertain to the street demonstration. Almost as if it were a reiteration of the project of Eleanor

18

Marx, militant translator, who imagined 'the languages of the international' as a set of codes and gestures capable of making words, customs and political styles mutually comprehensible.

Without a doubt, in this desire for theory, there is strategy and a form of transnational existence that makes mass pedagogy into a concern of the first order. In this light, we also acknowledge the reactionary alarm that transforms the language, content and form of education into their preferred forum for attack and counter-offensive. One of the central sites of this reaction is the combat against so-called 'gender ideology'.

As Sonia Correa argues, gender ideology is a 'catch-all' or multi-headed 'hydra' term that brings together – as targets of attack – the language of gender, study programmes in schools and universities, media content, laws for the right to abortion and sexual and reproductive rights more broadly, as well as attacks on leading transfeminist intellectuals and theological debates.[13] The fact that the word 'ideology' is the common thread in this series of political questions – or to put it another way, that it is the term underpinning a 'conservative political economy' – allows us to read against the grain the formative, intellectual and pedagogical heft of the work undertaken by the transfeminist movements. And it is this dispute that I have sought to call here, seeking its contours, a desire for theory.[14]

Translated from Spanish (Argentine) by Fionn Petch

Notes

1. Verónica Gago, *La puissance féministe: Ou le désir de tout changer* [*Feminist Power: Or, the Desire to Change Everything*], trans. Léa Nicolas-Teboul (Paris: Éditions Divergences, 2021).
2. Judith Butler, *What World Is This? A Pandemic Phenomenology* (New York: Columbia University Press, 2022), 43.
3. See Luci Cavallero and Verónica Gago, *La casa como laboratorio: Finanzas, vivienda y trabajo esencial* [*The Home as Laboratory: Finance, Housing and Essential Work*] (Buenos Aires: Tinta Limón / CLACSO, 2022).

FEMINISM FOR THE WORLD

4. Comisión Económica para América Latina y el Caribe (CEPAL), in its report *Panorama Social de América Latina y el Caribe 2022*. See Press release of 24 November 2022: 'Poverty Rates in Latin America Remain above Pre-Pandemic Levels in 2022, ECLAC Warns', www.cepal.org/en/pressreleases/poverty-rates-latin-america-remain-above-pre-pandemic-levels-2022-eclac-warns.

5. Quoted in Paul Frölich, *Rosa Luxemburg: Her Life and Work* (London: Pluto Press, 1972), 124.

6. bell hooks, *Feminist Theory: From Margin to Center* (London: Pluto Press, 2000), xiii.

7. Ibid.

8. See Maria Mies, *Patriarchy and Accumulation on a World Scale: Women in the International Division of Labour* (London: Zed Books, 1986).

9. See Silvia Federici, *Revolution at Point Zero: Housework, Reproduction, and Feminist Struggle* (New York: PM Press, 2020).

10. Julieta Kirkwood, *Preguntas que hicieron movimiento: Escritos feministas, 1979–1985* [*Questions Which Made a Difference: Feminist Writings, 1979–1985*] (Santiago: Banda Propia, 2021).

11. Vladimir I. Lenin, 'On Slogans', *Lenin Collected Works*, Vol. 25 (Moscow: Progress Publishers, 1977), 185.

12. LasTesis, *Set Fear on Fire: The Feminist Call that Set the Americas Ablaze* (London: Verso, 2023).

13. Sonia Correa, 'Gender Ideology', CREA Conference, 2019, https://sxpolitics.org/sonia-correa-gender-ideology-for-2019-crea-conference/19737.x

14. Translator's note: below are some further references that did not appear in the original version of the article: Verónica Gago, *Feminist International: How to Change Everything* (London: Verso, 2020); Silvia Riversa Cusicanqui, *Ch'ixinakax utxiwa: On Decolonising Practices and Discourses*, trans. Molly Geidel (Cambridge: Polity Press, 2020); Rita Laura Segato and Ramsey McGlazer, 'A Manifesto in Four Themes'. *Critical Times* 1(1) (2018): 198–211. https://doi.org/10.1215/26410478-1.1.198; Raquel Gutiérrez Aguilar, *In Defense of Common Life: The Political Thought of Raquel Gutiérrez-Aguilar*, ed. Brian Whitener and trans. J.D. Pluecker, (Matawan: Common Notions, 2024); Mina Lorena Navarro Trujillo, 'Saber-hacer ecofeminista para vivir-y-morir-con en tiempos del capitaloceno: luchas de mujeres contra los extractivismos en Abya Yala'. *Bajo el Volcán: Revista del Posgrado de Sociología* 3(5) (2021–2022); and Josefina Ludmer, *Aquí América latina: Una especulación* (Buenos Aires: Eterna Cadencia Editora, 2010).

2
The Collection 'Femmes en luttes de tous les pays'
A Political Publishing Story (1970–1980)

Françoise Vergès

In the years 1970–1980, in Europe, revolutionary internationalism mobilised on multiple fronts, with struggles against fascist regimes in Portugal and in Spain, and against the military dictatorship in Greece – a reminder that the Allied victory hadn't put an end to fascism and that supposedly democratic and liberal Europe tolerated these governments. Meanwhile, it demonstrated solidarity with anti-colonial and anti-imperialist struggles in Vietnam, Laos and Cambodia, against the military coups, dictatorships and reigns of terror supported by the CIA in Central and South America, against military interventions in Africa and the neocolonial policies of the French state overseas. While the links between fascism, the state, militarism and imperialism were subject to new examination, the dissemination of writings by theorists and militants in these struggles became ever more urgent. At the heart of feminist movements in the Global North, debate raged over the legitimacy of taking up arms, some criticising the masculine drive inherent in choosing weapons as contrary to feminist values, while others defended women who chose to wield them,[1] seeing in the torture, imprisonment, assassination and disappearance of female militants, and the use of rape as torture and as a weapon of war, an indissoluble connection between misogyny and domination.

In France, groups from the Mouvement de libération des femmes (Women's Liberation Movement, MLF) joined these efforts and published in their journals and magazines texts on women's actions in anti-fascist and anti-imperial struggles. While refraining from proclaiming an abstract sisterhood in which all women share the same interests and same forms of struggle, this feminist internationalism encouraged, supported and accompanied anti-racist, anti-capitalist, anti-fascist and anti-imperial struggles as it sought to depatriarchalise them. It simultaneously expressed itself through concrete actions: the organisation of international meetings, petitions, publications, setting up secret refuges and sanctuaries, making documentary films, providing financial support, adopting the children of assassinated militants, protecting from repression, sharing information, supporting prisoners, victims of torture and families of the disappeared – and developing and circulating theories and analyses. It interrogated the machismo of revolutionary movements, fostered versions of history that gave voice to the 'anonymous' and to collectives, and sought to produce its own representations of these stories. For feminists, anti-imperialist solidarity became an imperative, and translating and circulating texts was seen as a necessity. In France, we can enumerate as many as thirteen dedicated collections of writings from 1973 to 1978 published by major publishers. While all are linked by the abstract category of 'women', the *Éditions des femmes* (literally, 'women's publishing house') founded in 1974, announced its intentions more clearly with the launch of the collection 'Femmes en luttes de tous les pays' ('Women in struggle from every country'). This is the publishing policy we will explore here.

THE COLLECTION 'FEMMES·EN LUTTES DE TOUS LES PAYS'

In April 1974, the female founders of *Éditions des femmes* declared that their objective was to stand against capitalist and 'phallocratic' publishing enterprises and to 'publish the rejects of bourgeois publishers'.[2] Who were these rejects where it concerns the collection 'Femmes en luttes de tous les pays'? Among the list of 41 titles in the collection on the publisher's website,[3] *Amazon Odyssey* (Ti-Grace Atkinson, 1975) and *Three Guineas* (Virginia Woolf, 1977) rub shoulders with texts by militants from the Global South, which to my eyes illustrates the fascination of the collection. Of them, eight present a distinctive cover design: a small, square colour photograph (usually showing a group of women) beneath which the collection title *femmes en luttes de tous les pays* appears in italics, followed by the book title in red cursive script, with a subtitle in black below it. To the bottom left is the publisher's name *des femmes*, followed by a black line beneath which appear, at the very bottom right, the words 'pour chacune' – 'for each woman'. Most often, the names of the militants who have gathered the testimonies published in the collection don't appear on the front cover, nor on the back cover, nor inside.[4] This was a time when most feminist groups rejected the idea of individual signatures in their journals and reviews. The idea of personalising a work perceived and experienced as collective wouldn't have occurred to them.[5]

Among the works in this collection, I'd like to mention *Mujeres de Nicaragua* by Paz Espejo (1980), *Tupamaras: Des femmes de l'Uruguay* by Ana Maria Araujo (1980), *El Salvador: Une femme du front de libération témoigne* by Ana Guadalupe Martínez (1981), *Lettres à une idiote espagnole* and *Enfers* by Lidia Falcón, and *Chilenas: Des Chiliennes. Des femmes en luttes au Chili* by Carmen Gloria Aguayo de Sota (1981), to which I would add Eva Forest, *Diario y cartas desde la carcel. Journal et lettres de prison*, which appeared in 1975 in another *des femmes* collection.[6] I have selected here the titles that most directly

23

evoke problems that remain pertinent today: their authors ask how to resist state repression and how to face torture. They fight a racial capitalism that manufactures lives that don't count, mostly indigenous, Black and racialised women. They consider how to mobilise more widely against imperialist militarism. They underscore the importance of analysing the causes of a defeat or facing up to the risks that follow a victory, and emphasise the hardships of living in hiding or in exile. Finally, they draw attention to all the divisions and personal feelings of abandonment and isolation that can beset activists and the struggles themselves. The rejection or suppression that the authors confront concerns a political feminist theory of torture, of prison and of the armed liberation struggle. At a time when racial neoliberal capitalism and the climate crisis it has provoked, as well as militarism, pose burning questions for anti-racist and decolonial feminists, the history of this suppression and the manner in which it was interrogated in 1970–1980 are of considerable interest.

These texts interrogate a Western, pacifist feminism that does not consider class relations at the heart of its analyses, doesn't see imperialism as its principal enemy, and does not treat national liberation as an imperative. Challenging a liberal internationalism that presupposes an abstract universal sisterhood, the authors of these works and the women whose words they gather assert an internationalism that defends national sovereignty as well as transnational solidarity. There is still no mention of homophobia and lesbophobia within armed groups, the rights of indigenous peoples are only partially addressed in *Mujeres de Nicaragua*, and the structural racism and whiteness in Central and South America are never touched on. The faith in the righteousness of the popular struggles expressed in these works can appear quaint but it comes on the back of decades of attacks on the national liberation struggles and the promotion of neoliberal individualism. By contrast,

THE COLLECTION 'FEMMES EN LUTTES DE TOUS LES PAYS'

the analyses of government authoritarianism that emerge from these struggles – of their whiteness, their sexism, misogyny and homophobia, or their submission to neoliberalism – have renewed the field of feminist theories on anti-imperialism, structural racism and patriarchalisation.[7]

I would like to open a parenthesis here to point out that referring to the *des femmes* publishing house by means of one of its collections also obliges us to confront the criticisms made of those who founded it, namely, the Psychanalyse et Politique ('Psy et Po') group and Antoinette Fouque. It is quite legitimate to examine the origins of *des femmes*, the source of the capital that financed the trips, the meetings, the creation and promotion of multiple enterprises – bookshops, journals, reviews, publications – and to question the editorial choices and the role of Antoinette Fouque in all of this. The critical and materialist (but not moralist) analysis of the role of personal fortunes or state funding for social or revolutionary movements forms an undeniable part of their history.[8] However, it is the book production that I wish to address here. Publishing is a political gesture and editorial policies have a significant impact. We need only think of the policies maintained by Éditions François Maspero and Éditions de Minuit in the second half of the twentieth century. It is no surprise that they were targeted by state censorship. Likewise, it is no surprise to observe, in recent times, the attempts by multibillionaires with openly reactionary positions to seize television channels, radio stations, publishing houses and other distribution channels, or that we are witnessing the state looking for ways to restrict opinions that are contrary to its policies by threatening to dissolve movements or by attacking theories (decolonial, gender, etc.). The dissemination of anti-capitalist, anti-imperialist, abolitionist and decolonial ideas has always represented a danger for the bourgeois state.

To my mind, the phenomenon that is represented by the collection 'Femmes en luttes de tous les pays' only lasted a couple of decades. By the end of the 1980s, state and civic feminism had found a firmer foothold at the national and international levels. And the fierce ideological struggles within the MLF, rekindled by the appropriation of the acronym by Psy et Po in 1979, drove women away from the movement. Many activists suffered from indifference to their specific conditions, and from the vertical hierarchy and violence that could govern relations within feminist groups. Such struggles were very heated, as the debates revealed strong differences in theoretical and practical approaches to social and political liberation, as well as in the conception of priorities in these struggles. These differences should only come as a surprise to those who have a naive vision of political movements and believe in an illusory, abstract sisterhood. To imagine that debates within feminist movements should naturally be serene because they involve women is to deny the importance of the ideas and the emotional investment made in the goals of liberation.

Meanwhile, external events impacted on the social movements. In France, the election of François Mitterand as president in 1981 opened up career opportunities to feminists while the adoption of the 'tournant de la rigueur' (austerity turn) led to privatisations and closures of factories that particularly affected women (in the textile and homeware sectors), who lost their jobs or had to turn to working for subcontractors. The suppression of France's colonial past, the adoption of anti-racist movements by the Socialists, the advancement of racist anti-migration policies, the triumph of state neoliberalism with the victories of Thatcher and Reagan transformed the field of struggle, which also saw the emergence of new forms of conflict. For example, the struggle of AIDS sufferers against the stigmatisation and abandonment they suffered at the hands of governments that let them die. Over the course of

THE COLLECTION 'FEMMES EN LUTTES DE TOUS LES PAYS'

these years of neoliberal onslaught that struck so hard against working-class and racialised women, *des femmes* played no part in the critique of capitalism and structural racism, and the feminist publishing houses did not suffer direct attacks by the state. The momentum around the collection 'Femmes en luttes de tous les pays' dissipated as it stubbornly adhered to a feminism that failed to criticise its own colonial character. While solidarity with women's struggles against fascism and European authoritarianism, against sexual and gender-based violence, and against dictatorships was expressed in several of the publications, this collection failed to address French republican coloniality, the aftermath of slavery and colonialism, and structural racism.[9]

In the late 1970s and early 1980s, I myself had no hesitation in taking with me to Réunion copies of *Journal et lettres de prison* by Eva Forest (1975), *Mujeres de Nicaragua* by Paz Espejo (1980), *Tupamaras* by Ana Maria Araujo (1980), *El Salvador: Une femme du front de libération témoigne* by Ana Guadalupe Martínez (1981), *Chilenas* by Carmen Gloria Aguayo de Sota (1982), *Sitt Marie Rose* by Etel Adnan (1978), or *Femmes, race et classe* by Angela Davis (1983). I took them for the Union des femmes de La Réunion (UFR), which displayed them on their stand at the annual party for the journal of the island's communist party, *Témoignages*, held each December. I brought books that could have been published by decolonial feminists on Réunion if French coloniality hadn't systematically hindered the island's autonomous development, and thereby the development of committed local publishing houses. What's more, I even saved on the cost of having them sent from France. In the eyes of these readers in Réunion, these works did not defend 'a differentialist logic that places women on the side of the protection and culture of life, and that based solidarity with women political prisoners on the defence of a "female" culture'.[10] They had their own interpretation, and knew per-

27

fectly well that solidarity with women in struggle did not rely on a 'female culture'. The struggles they waged on Réunion had hardened them. Their interpretation was not dependent on the personality of Antoinette Fouque.

Antifascism and feminisms

In 1975, 'Femmes en luttes de tous les pays' published books by Lidia Falcón and Eva Forest, two militants who had been kidnapped, tortured and imprisoned in Franco's jails. Falcón, the daughter of communist militants, an anti-Franco lawyer and militant, was arrested in September 1974 as she prepared a feminist assembly in Spain.[11] *Lettres à une idiote espagnole* ('Letters to a Spanish Idiot'), written in prison, speaks of the oppression of women in all spheres of society. The 'idiot' is her friend Eva Forest, using the term affectionately to describe her mistake at standing up to Francoism. The letters comprising the book end with a war cry – 'War on death, on lies, on hypocrisy, on stupidity, on dishonesty, on abuse... War on the exploiters! War, Eva!' – that shows that this 'idiocy' comprises a radical attack on a country torn apart by terror and torture.

In *Enfers*, meanwhile, Falcón revisits the conditions of detention at Yeserias, the women's prison in Madrid, and gives voice to both political and ordinary prisoners. This position is in line with the anti-prison struggles that rejected any such distinction: all detained women are political prisoners because it is patriarchal capitalism that declares they have committed 'crimes'. Falcón dedicates *Enfers* to 'women in a man's world of boots, guns, gates, shouts, roars, crude laughter, obscene jokes' and notes that 'the heroes are in men's prisons. We don't write the sagas of women prisoners and martyrs. The press, literature, cinema all ignore them. They don't give rise to questions in parliament, nor demonstrations, nor assemblies.' She, who has 'seen the corridors of hell', claims to have

The Collection 'Femmes en luttes de tous les pays'

'been in close and painful contact with misery, forgetting, illness, madness, frustrated maternal impulse, undernourished infancy, silence, blindness, wounds and death, in intimate and close proximity to sacrifice, love and friendship.'[12]

Diario y cartas desde la carcel. Journal et lettres de prison comprises the diary of Eva Forest and the letters she wrote to her children while she was recovering from the torture she had suffered.[13] Accused, along with fifteen of her comrades, of complicity in attacks on dignitaries of the fascist regime, Eva Forest was arrested on 25 September 1974, tortured and held incommunicado for nine days in the premises of the Dirección General de Seguridad, run by Franco's police and from which, in the words of Alejandro Diz, a member of FRAP (Frente Revolucionario Antifascista y Patriota) who had seen the inside of it himself, one only emerged 'feet first or, if you were lucky, in a very poor condition'.[14] In the introduction, Forest writes that 'this is a *circumstantial* book. A pretext book, to draw attention to a collective problem, a *book of solidarity*, in short.'[15] In France, in light of the threat of death sentences for militants by Franco's tribunals, this solidarity was growing. On 5 October 1975, MLF groups called a women's gathering at Hendaye, on the Spanish border: 'Five men have just been murdered by Franco, the oldest friend of Hitler and Mussolini... It is urgent, and time presses. There are women and men still alive in prison. Our strength, our determination, our love must save them.'[16]

The publication of *Journal et lettres de prison*, which forms one expression of this solidarity, was not unanimously supported by Basque and Spanish prisoners and activists. They criticised the defence of political prisoners as 'women', and the attention granted to Falcón and Forest was seen as disregarding the situation of working-class women prisoners.[17] Anti-Franco militants mistrusted a feminism they saw as bourgeois, that did not support armed struggle and did not give enough consideration to the importance of class struggle.[18] Furthermore, the way in which fascism specifically targeted women hadn't been fully formulated, and the participation of women in armed struggles was still the subject of debate. The concept of 'sexual fascism', forged 'from testimonies of torture suffered by women', did not appear until 1976 'in the magazine *Vindicación feminista*.'[19] It was to be discussed at the 'International Tribunal for Crimes against Women in Brussels, convened in 1976 and attended by a Spanish delegation (including a women's representative from FRAP, Lidia Falcón), [which] provided both a forum for hearing testimonies and a framework for developing conceptual tools describing how dictatorial violence was embedded in patriarchal logics.'[20]

'Women's struggle is a global struggle':[21] *Imperialism and feminisms*

In 1980 and 1981, there appeared in the collection four books on women's participation in armed struggles in Central and South America, recounting the obstacles that the female militants encountered, such as machismo within the movements, the reactionary weight of the Church, as well as links between Catholicism and Marxism, sexuality, maternity in prison or in hiding, exile, reasons for defeat or victory, and new challenges arising once combat was over. These titles were: *Mujeres de Nicaragua: Des femmes du Nicaragua*; *Tupamaras: Des femmes de l'Uruguay*; *El Salvador: Une femme du Front de Libération témoigne*; and *Chilenas: Des Chiliennes*.[22] For their authors, these books are 'the result of a collective and militant effort', and form 'part of a specific experience that all those involved in revolutionary actions should discuss and analyse'.[23]

They all considered the formation of an army of liberation to be a necessity because the governing classes rejected all

THE COLLECTION 'FEMMES EN LUTTES DE TOUS LES PAYS'

forms of democracy and the militias of the large landowners and the death squads exercised a reign of terror.

> Each day, in the morning, on the roads, on public tips, we find bodies with their eyes gouged out, tortured, cut up while alive, decapitated, subjected to the most abominable torments before they died. Teachers were murdered simply because they had joined a trade union. The barbarity is such that an activist is no longer afraid of dying, but lives in fear of being captured alive.[24]

'The participation of women in the armed struggle shattered the myth of their passivity and non-violence.'[25] They have all shown enormous courage, and earned their rights where 'having "balls" played no decisive role at all'.[26] They also challenged sexism and the patriarchy within movements, limited to gendered roles, whether desexualised or hypersexualised.[27] When arrested, the police treated them as unworthy of being treated as 'women', while at the same time they were humiliated as women, immediately stripped naked, threatened with rape, raped, deprived of water for washing, of menstrual pads, of clothing. 'Every time I wanted to go to the toilet, I had to ask [...] They'd untie me from the gas cylinder and stand there watching me. I couldn't even urinate in peace. I couldn't see them because I was blindfolded, but I could hear all their obscenities.'[28] In prison, they endured hunger, thirst, torture, depression, illness. This didn't stop them organising a prison university, supporting each other, striking to improve conditions. They were conscious that 'there will be advances and setbacks, as in every struggle... But there will also be a great deal of lucidity, of love, and a deep revolutionary conviction.'[29]

Whether a 'Comandante' like Ana Guadalupe Martínez, or soldiers or militants like those interviewed in *Chilenas*,

Tupamaras or *Mujeres de Nicaragua*, all express a defiance towards a European feminism that is not anti-capitalist or which, due to its rigid view of secularity, rejects the importance of liberation theology or the role of Afro-descendant or Indigenous spiritualities. Their feminisms do not follow the same paths.[30] They denounce the sexism of iconic leaders such as Che Guevara,[31] while celebrating the fact he spoke of 'revolutionary love in a continent of violence'.[32] They question the natalist politics of the Latin American left and of governments when the reality is one of 'kids fainting with hunger in school, kids without shoes, pregnant women in a state of severe malnutrition'.[33] They note that the theoretical and political contributions made by women in prison was never sought nor taken into account. Raking over the causes of a defeat or a failed armed operation, they engage in militant and political self-criticism. 'The women's struggle is a global struggle, because it calls into question the totality of human beings, their social relations, their education and their sexuality, with a strength and violence capable of subverting the entire system.'[34]

Exile and underground resistance are at the heart of *Chilenas*. In the preface, Ana Vasquez, exiled in France since the CIA-supported military coup of 11 September 1973, revisits the *Centros de Madres* (Mothers' Centres), the organisations that, in her words, met with reticence on the part of Chilean militant groups that saw them as 'disguised charity, paternalism, a depoliticised movement'.[35] She sees in this rejection a refusal by the Marxist left where 'there was a fairly widespread view that women's problems could be explained by the class struggle, relegating them as a secondary contradiction'.[36] The third part of the book brings together the testimonies of women who held a clandestine meeting on 12 and 13 December 1981 in a convent on the outskirts of Santiago, under the pretext of a religious retreat and under

THE COLLECTION 'FEMMES EN LUTTES DE TOUS LES PAYS'

the protection of the Mother Superior and the nuns.[37] These testimonies were collected by two Psy et Po activists who had been invited to attend, and who then went on to visit women's groups in the *poblaciones* (communities), again in secret.[38]

Rereading these books 40 years later reveals to what extent the dismantling of racial capitalism and imperialisms is a long-term struggle. In 1990, ten years after the publication of the book by Ana Guadalupe Araujo and while the war was still underway, myself and two other militants were invited to El Salvador by Mujeres por la Vida y la Dignidad, where I was able to testify that her analyses remained relevant. The group wanted us to gather witness accounts of women fighting against the war financed by US imperialism. The Salvadoran army and CIA-backed militias were responsible for torture, deaths and massacres, and Mujeres por la Vida y la Dignidad wanted to denounce sexual and racist abuse. Faced with the death squads who enjoyed total impunity, they reminded us that sexual fascism remains the source of a racist and sexist politics, while its activists developed a politics of life and dignity.[39]

In this quick sketch of an editorial policy within the MLF in the years 1970–1980, we see the shape of a feminist revolution emerging that is anti-patriarchal, anti-racist, anti-capitalist and anti-imperialist, of which the women's strike in Argentina, for example, may be seen as a contemporary expression. However, these feminisms were and continue to be shot through with conflicts and contradictions. The betrayals of the struggles of those years, the setbacks and defeats, do not erase the knowledge, the memories or the analyses that emerged from them. And anti-imperialist feminism remains essential. Today, the struggles against the occupation of Palestine, solidarity with the feminist revolution in Iran, with women's struggles in India, Turkey, Ukraine, Canada, Brazil, Argentina, South Africa, Algeria, Kurdistan and everywhere else are much better known. Criticism of civilisational feminism, feminationalism and pinkwashing is widespread. Afro-feminists, queer feminists, transfeminists, Islamic feminists, Muslim feminists, indigenous feminists, anti-racist feminists and environmentalist feminists are dynamically renewing debates on feminist theory and practice for liberation. Struggles against sexist and sexual violence have opened up a new field of conflict, abolitionist feminism clashes with prison feminism, and movements against environmental racism question a white ecology. The COVID-19 pandemic and police violence returned structural violence to the spotlight, highlighting that Black and racialised women are a majority in the jobs most exposed to the disease, to class and race injustices in relation to health, and to violence. Women refugees and migrants open up new frontlines, and contradictions are emerging, testifying that no political struggle ever unfolds against a harmonious backdrop. Today, the profusion of titles and translations demonstrates the continued hunger for publishing policies that allow us to better understand different feminist theories and to gain a deeper understanding of the forms taken by women's struggles around the globe – in order to reinvigorate an authentic internationalism of struggles and ideas.

Translated from French by Fionn Petch

Notes

1. This debate also examined the presence of women in armed groups in France, Italy and Germany in the 1970s and 1980s. See Ulrike Meinhof, *Mutinerie et autres textes. Déclarations et analyses des militants de la Fraction armée rouge emprisonnés à Stammheim* [*Mutiny and Other Texts. Statements and Analyses by Red Army Faction Activists Imprisoned in Stammheim*] (Paris: Éditions des femmes, 1977); and Fanny Bugnon, '*Quand le militantisme fait le choix des armes: les femmes d'Action directe et les médias*' ['When Militancy

THE COLLECTION 'FEMMES EN LUTTES DE TOUS LES PAYS'

Takes Up Arms: The Women of Direct Action and the Media'],
Sens public, 2009, https://doi.org/10.7202/1064239ar.

2. Quoted in Bibia Pavard, '*Femmes, politique et culture: les premières années des Éditions des femmes (1972–1979)*' ['Women, Politics and Culture: The First Years of Éditions des femmes (1972–1979)'], *Bulletin Archives du féminisme* 8 (December 2004), www.archivesdufeminisme.fr/sommaires-des-bulletins/bulletin-08/pavard-b-femmes-politique-culture-les-premieres-annees-editions-femmes-1972-1979/. Pavard recalls that in 1972 a 'publishing group' was set up within Psychanalyse et Politique (Psy et Po) to consider this project. An insert published in *Le Torchon Brûle*, the journal of the Mouvement de libération, stated: 'There are a certain number of us who want to try and publish the texts we write ourselves.' The publishing house would not be 'that of the MLF but that of women', its creators stated at the Lutetia press conference in 1974. Little by little, the collective organisation was replaced by a vertical and hierarchical organisation.

3. 'Essais Luttes de femmes', Antoinette Fouque, *des femmes*, consulted April 2023, www.desfemmes.fr/rubrique-essais/luttes-de-femmes/.

4. This is the case, for example, with *Chilenas* (1982) and *Femmes et Russie* [*Women and Russia*] (1980), whose testimonies were collected by Psy et Po activists.

5. This is a policy pursued today by feminist groups such as Mwasi, Les Locs, Pride Banlieue, feminist collage activists and queer groups. It also remains the policy of militant groups like Les Soulèvements de la Terre. By changing its name to 'des femmes: Antoinette Fouque', the publishing house abandoned this policy, and a work that had been collective became personalised.

6. Translator's Note: all of these texts were translated by the translation collective of éditions des femmes, including Paz Espejo, *Des femmes du Nicaragua* [*Women of Nicaragua*] (Paris: des femmes, 1980); Ana Maria Araujo, *Tupamaras: Des femmes de l'Uruguay* [*Tupamaras: Women of Uruguay*] (Paris: des femmes, 1980); Ana Guadalupe Martínez, *El Salvador: Une femme du front de libération témoigne* [*El Salvador: Testimony of a Woman on the Liberation Front*] (Paris: des femmes, 1981); Lidia Falcón, *Lettres à une idiote*

35

espagnole [*Letters to a Spanish Idiot*] (Paris: des femmes, 1975), and *Enfers* [*Hell*] (Paris: des femmes, 1979); Femmes en luttes de tous les pays Collective and Carmen Gloria Aguayo de Sota, *Chilenas: Des Chiliennes. Des femmes en luttes au Chili* [*Women in Struggle in Chile*] (Paris: des femmes, 1981); and Eva Forest, *Diario y cartas desde la carcel: Journal et lettres de prison* [*Diary and Letters from Prison*] (Paris: des femmes, 1975).

7. Ana Maria Araujo, in *Tupamaras*, is probably the one who takes this self-criticism the furthest.

8. Historically, social and revolutionary movements have received financial support from wealthy individuals. They have also invented other sources of income: membership fees for activists, strike funds, collections of donations, the creation of cooperative enterprises, the sale of newspapers, artistic works and other products. They have also staged bank heists. But this support has never reached the level of funding that billionaires give to reactionary or far-right movements, think tanks, lobbying companies or consultancies that finance anti-abortion, anti-migrant, anti-gay or anti-union campaigns.

9. Feminist magazines reported on women's struggles in Guadeloupe and Martinique, but feminist publishing did not reflect them. In 1982, Tierce did publish a book on a domestic workers' union (1982), but it was based in South America. With *Femmes arabes et sœurs musulmanes* [*Arab Women and Muslim Sisters*] by Denise Brahimi (1984), *Sexe, Idéologie, Islam* by Fatima Mernissi (1987) and *Continents noirs* [*Black Continents*] by Awa Thiam (1987), Tierce introduced non-European feminist issues that did not relate to French coloniality in its overseas territories. These books were published by L'Harmattan.

10. Irène Gimenez, '*Les prisonnières politiques ne sont-elles pas des femmes? Construire des solidarités féministes transnationales avec les prisonnières politiques en sortie de dictature (État espagnol, années 1970–1980)*' ['Are Political Prisoners Not Women? Building Transnational Feminist Solidarity with Women Political Prisoners Emerging from Dictatorships (The Spanish State, 1970s–1980s)'], in Natacha Chetcuti-Osorovitz and Sandrine Sanos (eds), *Le genre carcéral: Pouvoir disciplinaire, agentivité et expériences de la prison du*

THE COLLECTION 'FEMMES EN LUTTES DE TOUS LES PAYS'

xix⁴ au xxi⁴ siècle [*The Prison Genre: Disciplinary Power, Agentivity, and Prison Experiences from the Nineteenth to the Twenty-First Century*] (Gif-sur-Yvette: Éditions des maisons des sciences de l'homme associées, 2022).

11. On Lidia Falcón, see Allison Taillot, '*Féminisme et générations en Espagne: le féminisme génétique de Lidia Falcón*' ['Feminism and Generations in Spain: Lidia Falcón's Genetic Feminism'], in Éric Fisbach and Philippe Rabaté (eds), *HispanismeS*, no. 8 (2016), https://hispanistes.fr/images/PDF/HispanismeS/Hispanismes_8/13_Taillot_Allison_HispanismeS_8.pdf. Founder of the Feminist Party of Spain in 1981, then of feminist newspapers, Lidia Falcón has published numerous books and plays. In 2019, she was sued by the Federación Plataforma Trans (Trans Platform Federation), which accused her of hate speech because she opposed the administration of puberty blockers and the penalisation of parents who refuse to affirm the self-identified gender identity of their children. See Lidia Falcón, 'Women Are Being Erased from the Law and Public Policy', *WPUK*, 13 December 2020, https://womansplaceuk.org/2020/12/13/lidia-falcon-women-erased-from-the-law-and-public-policy/.

12. In *Le quotidien des femmes* [*Women's Daily Lives*], a magazine launched by *des femmes*. The publishing house also published Eva Forest's *Témoignages de lutte et de résistance* [*Testimonies of Struggle and Resistance*] (1978).

13. The front and back covers feature two drawings by her daughter, Eva. They show a river, free-roaming horses, bright sunshine and, surrounded by a wall, a building with bars on the windows, whose entrance is guarded by a man in uniform and on which is written 'Prision'. At the end of the book, there is a testimony by Maria Luz Fernandez, a 23-year-old schoolteacher who spent 114 days incommunicado in Franco's police headquarters, and a reproduction of a handwritten letter from Eva Forest.

14. Isabelle Galichon, 'Le devenir-victime d'Eva Forest face à la torture' [Eva Forest's Victimhood in the Face of Torture'], *Nuevo Mundo Mundos Nuevos*, Questions du temps présent, online since 11 June 2015, http://journals.openedition.org/nuevomundo/67997.

FEMINISM FOR THE WORLD

15. Eva Forest, *Diario y cartas desde la carcel: Journal et lettres de prison*, 11, emphasis in the original. In this prologue, she also recalled that reading a petition for solidarity in *Le Monde* on 23 October 1974 had been 'one of the first breaths of optimism to reach us from outside'. An advertisement signed by thousands of women from different countries had been purchased in *Le Monde*.

16. Quoted by Nalu Faria, '*Féminisme internationaliste et solidaire pour renverser l'autoritarisme*' ['International Feminism Solidarity to Overthrow Authoritarianism'], *Capire*, 1 October 2021. See also the documentaries by Carole Roussopoulos and Ioana Wieder, *La Marche des femmes à Hendaye* (Vidéo Out/Les Muses s'amusent, 1975), and *Manifestation à Hendaye, 5 octobre 1975* (Vidéo Out/Les Muses s'amusent, 1975). These documentaries, based on the same footage, can be consulted at the Bibliothèque nationale de France, NUMAV-661333 s.

17. Gimenez, '*Les prisonnières politiques ne sont-elles pas des femmes?*'

18. Some feminists criticised support for the armed struggle in Spain and wrote 'the wide range of left-wing political forces that consider armed violence to be a mistake at the present time, including among which, of course, is the feminist movement', quoted by Gimenez, '*Les prisonnières politiques ne sont-elles pas des femmes?*'

19. See Gila Claudia Jereno, '*La revue* Vindicación Feminista *(1976–1979) et le féminisme radical espagnol dans un contexte transnational: actrices, échanges et influences*' ['The Magazine *Vindicación Feminista* (1976–1979) and Spanish Radical Feminism in a Transnational Context: Actors, Exchanges and Influences'], PhD thesis in Spanish and Gender Studies, under the supervision of Mercedes Yusta Rodrigo and Pilar Díaz Sánchez, Université Paris 8 and Universidad Autónoma de Madrid, 2019; and Diana E.H. Russel and Nicole Van de Ven, *Crimes Against Women: Proceedings of the International Tribunal* (Berkeley, CA: Russell Publications, 1976 and 1990).

20. Gimenez, '*Les prisonnières politiques ne sont-elles pas des femmes?*'

21. Araujo, *Tupamaras*, 21.

22. Espejo, *Mujeres de Nicaragua*; Araujo, *Tupamaras*; Martínez, *El Salvador*; and Ana Vasquez, Préface, Femmes en luttes de tous les pays Collective and Carmen Gloria Aguayo de Sota, *Chilenas* (Paris: Éditions des femmes, 1982).

38

The Collection 'Femmes en luttes de tous les pays'

23. Martínez, *El Salvador*, 36.
24. Oscar Martinez Penate, *Le soldat et la guérillera: Une histoire orale de la guerre civile au Salvador* [*The Soldier and the Guerrillera: An Oral History of the Civil War in El Salvador*] (Paris: Syllepse, 2018), 14–26.
25. Araujo, *Tupamaras*, 258.
26. Espejo, *Mujeres de Nicaragua*, 80–81.
27. Ibid., 260 and 166.
28. Martínez, *El Salvador*, 74.
29. Ana-Maria Etcheverria, Preface to Ana Guadalupe Martínez, *El Salvador: Une femme du Front de Libération témoigne* [*El Salvador: Testimony of a Woman on the Liberation Front*] (Paris: Éditions des femmes, 1981), 31.
30. Araujo, *Tupamaras*, 22.
31. Ibid., 130–133.
32. Ibid., 128.
33. Femmes en luttes de tous les pays Collective and Aguayo de Sota, *Chilenas*, 196.
34. Araujo, *Tupamaras*, 21.
35. Femmes en luttes de tous les pays Collective and Aguayo de Sota, *Chilenas*, 20.
36. Ibid., 22–23.
37. Indeed, the army came to the convent, demanded to see the Mother Superior and to check that it was in fact a prayer retreat.
38. The two activists gave their tapes and photos to a French diplomat, who sent them to France in a diplomatic bag. They were then subjected to a full body search at the airport.
39. On our way to a village in the mountains, several hours from the capital, where women farmers had organised themselves into a cooperative, we were arrested by Salvadoran army officers. Suspected of giving aid to the FLMN, we were transferred to San Salvador prison and interrogated. Thanks to the immediate solidarity shown by Mujeres por la Vida y la Dignidad at the international and local level, we were released after two days, along with the Salvadorans accompanying us (a young woman and a young man), from whom we had been separated as soon as we were arrested and for whom we were very worried.

3

Motherhood from a Iabá Point of View

Djamila Ribeiro

For Exu, lord of the market

Introduction

An *itan* (or *itã*) is a text about the *orixás*, the divinities worshipped in Candomblé, the religion that originated among Yoruba people transported to Brazil from the region that today includes Nigeria, Benin and Togo. During centuries of slave trafficking into Brazil, Candomblé retained its roots but also overlaid them with a Brazilian identity. For example, the widely worshipped divinity Yemanjá originally came from Abeokuta, now part of Nigeria, where she reigned over freshwater sources. In Brazil, she has become the queen of the ocean, and bathes her sons and daughters in the saltwater swell.

Passed down from generation to generation, *itan*s can be thousands of years old. The stories link us to our ancestors; through them, we learn about our past and can take the measure of the present. For many sons and daughters of the *orixás*, the *itan*s are true stories: they really happened and led directly to our forebears' deification. For researchers with a professional interest in Candomblé, these stories together describe Yoruba mythology. The *itan*s' origins are wide-ranging and there are many variations within individual tales, almost as many as the

40

MOTHERHOOD FROM A IABÁ POINT OF VIEW

number of their tellers. Moreover, some *itan*s are much better known than others; some have been immortalised in the works of French anthropologists such as Pierre Verger,[1] while others are still only heard by initiates and frequenters of the *terreiros*, as they call the spaces where people gather to hear Candomblé liturgies. Some *itan*s are Brazilian natives and others hail from Cuba, but the majority survived the horrors of the transatlantic traffic to find a second home along the Brazilian coast, remaining vital by stitching different approaches together out of the wisdom of their elders.

The *itan*s form a powerful connection with the divine force of the natural world. According to one *itan* recorded in Reginaldo Prandi's book *Mitologia dos Orixás* (*Mythology of the Orixás*),[2] Yemanjá, a female *orixá* or *iabá* aligned with water, was born from the union between Obatalá, the sky, and Odudua, the earth. With her brother Aganju, the dry land, Yemanjá had a child named Orungã, and this child developed an incestuous love for his mother. One day, Orungã abducted his mother and raped her. In desperation, Yemanjá managed to break free and run away from her son, but he chased after her. Just as Orungã was about to catch her once more, Yemanjá collapsed in a dead faint. According to Prandi, when she fainted, 'Her body grew extraordinarily large, such that her various parts gradually became valleys and hills and mountain ranges. From her breasts, grown as vast as mountains, two rivers began to flow. These rivers eventually joined together to form one great lagoon, which itself eventually became the sea.' Next, Yemanjá's womb ruptured and so more *orixás* were born: Xangô, lord of justice; Ogum, the *orixá* of war; Oyá, lady of the storms and protector of women; and many others. 'Last to be born was Exu, the messenger *orixá*. Each of Yemanjá's children has his or her own story, and each has his or her specific powers,' as Prandi's account concludes.

As the mother of many *orixás* and also as 'queen of the sea', Yemanjá is much loved in Brazil. She rules over all the *oris*. Our *ori* is the *orixá* divinity in the form that resides in our minds; the word *ori* can in fact be translated as 'head' but also as 'fate'. We ask Yemanjá for tranquillity, for her to cleanse our *oris* and to guide our feet and also those of our loved ones onto the right paths. Worship of Yemanjá extends much further than disciples of African-origin religions for, as the most well-known African divinity in Brazil – and notwith-standing regular episodes of religious racism – every New Year's morning, on 1 January, we honour the established tra-dition of jumping seven waves at the start of a New Year's dip in the sea, in homage to the goddess and to bring good luck for the year to come. Ironically, perhaps because of her popu-larity among Christian groups, Yemanjá is widely depicted as a white woman, with long black hair and a blue tunic – very different from the Yemanjá who first set foot in Brazil, a full-breasted black woman. The African goddess's struggle for negritude remains a work-in-progress in Brazil and the topic resurfaces every year. As stated by Carla Akotirene:

> Yemonja is a mother. Iyabá [Queen of Mothers], it is she who forges women's beauty and their self-esteem, reflect-ing her own opulent black vanity, with her proud bosom: all non-European aesthetic markers. The mother of the waves enjoys receiving blossoms and lavender stems, while also duly feeding the sea with the signs of gratitude offered for the health of a person's *ori* (their head/mind) who did not succumb to moon-madness or go astray in the world of the moon, the guiding light of their ORIentation.
>
> Yemonja has influence during the low tides over any who may be moonstruck or completely lost amid this African diaspora with a broken history, in which the origins of our true names, our roots, the wealths of our seeds and our

MOTHERHOOD FROM A IABÁ POINT OF VIEW

inherited knowledge have been lost and transmuted into the colonisation of peoples and nature alike. I talk of these as lost minds in terms of their spiritual paths.[3]

The main celebrations of Yemanjá are held on 2 February, when crowds of the *povo de santo* or 'holy people' – as followers of African-origin religions are known in Brazil – fill the Rio Vermelho beach in Salvador, capital of the state of Bahia, bringing lavender and carnations and many other offerings to be launched in tiny boats and drift out into the sea. Worship of Yemanjá appears in classics of Bahian culture, including the novels of Jorge Amado and the songs of Dorival Caymmi and Maria Bethânia. Hymns to her flow unhindered by national frontiers and, throughout her history, Yemanjá has gloried in many alternative names. In Bantu traditions, the 2 February flowers are an offering to Dandalunda. In Umbanda, a Brazilian profession that combines the syncretism of African faiths with Christianity and indigenous beliefs, Yemanjá has many different names. Perhaps the best known in Brazil are Yara and Janaína.

The recent femicide case of Janaína Bezerra, a black journalism student at the federal university of Piauí ('UFPI') in Teresina (Piauí being one of Brazil's poorest states), had me thinking about the *itan* that describes the birth of Yemanjá's *orixá* children. The daughter of a bricklayer and a housewife, Janaína was the first in her family to go into higher education and she received one of the five highest scores for the entrance exam that year. Her mother said Janaína loathed macho men and that her dream had been to work in television. Janaína was found dead on the university campus, being carried by two students who were spotted by security personnel. She was covered in bruises and there was blood dripping from her crotch. The conclusion of the state's civil police was that Janaína had been raped twice and had her neck broken between

FEMINISM FOR THE WORLD

the first and second rapes. Later, in the course of further investigations, it was revealed that Janaína had collapsed in the early hours of the morning and been filmed covered in blood. Her death caused shock and turmoil at the university and throughout the state, prompting new policies for women's protection and to combat misogyny. So I offer my flowers in honour of Janaína,[4] who was lost, but whose loss, much like that of Yemanjá, has lent fuel to women's battle, powering our struggle and winning us renewed justice.

Seniority and female power in Candomblé

It's important to introduce Yemanjá to readers who may know very little or nothing at all about her, and perhaps less even about the liturgical traditions of Brazilian Candomblé. I think it's truly important that people of the Global North go beyond their standard references in the world; that we share our different systems of knowledge in an exchange that is essential for developing a richer understanding. In *The Invention of Women: Making an African Sense of Western Gender Discourses*, Oyèrónké Oyěwúmí pursues foundational work on thinking about gender from the starting point that the hierarchised opposition between men and women makes no sense within Yoruba logic, as evidenced by the language and specifically by its forms of address. For Oyěwúmí, notions of seniority and of respect due to older people, no matter their gender, are much more pertinent. The terms *iyá* (mother) and *babá* (father) are more meaningful than biological maternity or paternity, and instead indicate the position of the oldest person who, thanks to both their age and their life experiences, occupies an authority position in relation to younger people. As Oyěwúmí explains, 'No doubt gender has its place and time in scholarly analyses, but its place and its time were not precolonial Yoruba society.'[5]

MOTHERHOOD FROM A IABÁ POINT OF VIEW

In Brazil, for people with religions rooted in African systems, this relationship has taken a strong hold, in the context that the highest authority in the *terreiros* is the *iyalorixá* (holy mother) or *babalorixá* (holy father), effectively the priest or priestess of the cult. Old age, as practising *babalorixá* Rodney William Eugênio asserts,[6] takes on a different meaning for followers of Candomblé, as compared to the patriarchal Euro-Christian tradition, for it signifies both power and dignity. This is an old age that can also be called 'holy', and which generally begins from the moment of religious initiation.

Notwithstanding its precolonial Yoruba roots, Candomblé is Brazilian, the product of the syncretic practices of the vast numbers of enslaved peoples who were brought into the country. As such, it has particular foundation stories. According to one of these, among the earliest of our traditional *terreiros* that are still active today, the foremost religious leader has always been a woman. The names of celebrated *iyalorixás* such as Mãe Senhora, Mãe Menininha do Gantois, Mãe Stella de Oxóssi, among so many others, are written indelibly into the history of the religion. They are *mães de santo* or 'holy mothers' and so, if we are to talk about maternity in Candomblé, we must engage with the careers of our greatest female elders.

There is a range of reasons why these particular figures were appointed, creating the phenomenon of such widespread female leadership – a notable exception to men's historical dominance as repositories of religious power. These reasons are discussed by Teresinha Bernardo in her article 'Candomblé: Identities in Flux'. According to Bernardo, one reason is that a greater proportion of women in the nineteenth century were emancipated, compared to their male peers. Therefore, with a greater cohort of women pursuing their lives outside the plantations, black women could better filter into the society

45

around them, and so include in their activities the founding of Candomblé *terreiros*:

> As they were freed earlier and in greater numbers than their male peers, black women were able to move into the gaps that the world of free labour made available, becoming nannies, sweet-sellers and cooks, going out into the streets to sell their sweets, and sometimes eventually being able to buy their own friends' emancipation.[7]

Even so, the greater proportion of emancipation among women that Bernardo highlights would explain black women becoming heads of their families but not necessarily religious leaders. Indeed, there is scope to doubt this theory, for the majority of black women left slavery only to become domestic servants, a trajectory whose consequences are still playing out, with 5.7 million women working as servants in Brazil today, of whom 65 per cent are black. The race and gender divisions in the Brazilian workplace originate with the patriarchy, which makes it difficult to accept the proposal that black women had sufficient spare time and income to found Candomblé *terreiros*. As we follow up Bernardo's theory, we should look to the African diaspora in order to discover how black women came to assume leadership roles in the traditional *terreiros*, which continue even now under exclusively female leadership. In the slaves' hopelessness about ever returning home and their concomitant longing for their motherlands, Bernardo does identify a crucial influence on the enslaved society. According to her, Candomblé was conceived by women:

> primarily as a recreation of the homeland, the mother, the cave, nourishment and protection: all ultimately qualities attributed to the mother, and so demonstrating that there is no substantial difference between creator and creature, only

similarities. These qualities, common both to women and Candomblé, are entirely opposed to the authoritarianism and violence generated by any unifying rationale that does not permit pluralism of ideas.[8]

Although there are further depths to plumb here, Bernardo's idea of this shared significance offers a partial answer to our question. However, the mystery is still not fully accounted for, given that, prior to the *terreiros*, there were no models available for the creation of such spiritual spaces that also functioned as places of refuge for persecuted black communities. We need to recognise the courage and determination, the astounding creative resourcefulness of the women who went on to lead these spaces, despite the dominant and racist patriarchy. Geisimara Matos, biographer of Mãe Pulquéria, a formidable *iyalorixá* at the Gantois *terreiro*, evocatively describes these

> powerful black women presiding over the services, older and younger women all duly acknowledged and respected, occasionally feared, as much by their followers as by outsiders – people from all walks of life who quietly made sure to attend the Candomblé meetings, however hidden away, despite the practice running counter to the accepted behavioural norms of the time.[9]

To all of those witches, I offer my greatest respect.

Back to Yemanjá

As mother of the *orixás*, Yemanjá occupies a position of power. She is the 'lady of the household', not a 'housewife'; as the foremost mother in Candomblé, her maternal status is based not on her gender but on her advanced age and experience compared to that of her sons and daughters. Yemanjá's motherhood does not entail obligatory offers of hospitality nor restriction to the home. Her children enjoy a greater sense of control and authority over others around them, their authority emanating from Yemanjá herself as well as being reflected from the young people around her.

Another important part of the picture is that, within the Candomblé tradition, Yemanjá's status as a mother is very different from the Christian notion of the 'virgin' or 'immaculate' mother, that is, that of the woman who must not and indeed cannot feel pleasure, and who, if she does experience orgasm, must feel guilty. As the Mangueira samba school sang at Carnival 1973: 'I saw someone dive in, and never look back again'.[10]

Another *itan*, also recorded in Prandi's book, tells of how the supremely beautiful Yemanjá

one day left her home in the depths of the sea and went up onto dry land looking for pleasures of the flesh. She came across a handsome young fisherman and carried him away into her liquid love milk. Their bodies experienced all the joys of the encounter, but the fisherman was only a human and he died by drowning in his lover's arms. When the sun rose the next day, Yemanjá brought his body back to the beach.

And this is how it always goes, every night, when Yemanjá Conlá takes a fancy to the fishermen going out on their boats and rafts to work. She carries her chosen one down to the sea-bed, allows him to possess her, then brings him back, lifeless, to the shore.

Girlfriends and wives always run down at first light to the beach, to wait for the return of their menfolk who've been out to fish, and to implore Yemanjá to let them return alive. They bring the sea many gifts, many flowers, mirrors and perfumes, so that Yemanjá will always send plenty of fish and allow the fishermen to live.[11]

MOTHERHOOD FROM A IABÁ POINT OF VIEW

As Sueli Carneiro and Cristiane Abdon Cury point out,

> While patriarchal society reduces female sexuality to pro-
> creation alone, the African goddesses are both mothers
> and lovers. Yemanjá, mother of the *orixás*, enchants men
> and draws them into her great belly, the sea. She devours
> them because she is naturally changeable and ruled by her
> passions, both envious and possessive – indeed she *is* the
> sea, now calm and serene, now violent and destructive. She
> may reject her children, but she also loves them ardently.[12]

Working with these different knowledge systems is essential
if we are to broaden discussions about motherhood beyond
the strict focus on oppression, and engage with not one but
multiple modes of being a mother. Like the sea, our Yemanjá
is filled with meanings. On calm days as on stormy ones, she
accompanies all who navigate the seas, her dancing is led by
the moon's phases, and she offers many different seas of possibility for female being.

Yansã

There are other *iabás* in the pantheon of the *orixás* who present
other ways of mothering. Yansã, for example, has borne nine
children, but goes out to work every day, leaving the children
two ram's horns so that, should danger appear, they may beat
one horn against the other and she would return at the speed
of the wind. Many stories have been told, down the generations, about Yansã (also sometimes called Oyá), the *orixá* who
rules the storms. She can be as forceful as a herd of charging
buffalo, but also as peaceful and delicate as a cloud of butter-
flies. The women who follow Yansã have adopted her pride,
dignity and independence as they raise their own children
and create their own enterprises, whether as street-sellers of

acarajé fritters, as confectioners or nannies, whatever it takes this enslaved black people to resist. When Oyá goes by, she never goes unnoticed. She flicks the red of her dress all around the market, attracting everyone's attention. What's more, she sleeps with all the *orixás* and learns a secret from each of her partners. For example, from Xangô, her perfect partner, she learned to spit fire and so reign sovereign. As the traditional sayings go: 'to this woman whose dress is flames, none can tell a lie'. Oyá is the mistress of truth; she goes to war and leads the armies herself.

Like stormy weather, Oyá is often misunderstood, misjudged and maligned. But her daughters continue to lead armies and, in the process, they upset the status quo. Her behaviour and practice as a mother inspire many women, for hers is an approach that challenges the racist patriarchal logic consigning women to a single fate of domestic servitude and mothering romanticised in the form of constant availability at home to the children. Oyá defies the logic that would relegate women always to the service of men, to an ever-ready support in their careers; to being the one welcoming them home after a day's work with a hot supper and children ready for bed.

In fact, Yansá's skills encourage women to develop their own autonomy and strength, as many thousands of Brazilians indeed have done, as they lead their families in the search for sustenance and dignified lives.

Nanã Buruku

One of the *orixás* whose mothering I find most interesting is Nanã, the oldest *orixá* of them all, whose dominion over the original raw mud of life embodies her guardianship of the *orixás'* ancestral knowledge. Grandmother of the *orixás*, Nanã's realm is the marsh and mangrove swampland; and there was a time, as one *itan* tells, when she fell pregnant. She

MOTHERHOOD FROM A IABÁ POINT OF VIEW

gave birth to Omolu (also called Obaluaiyê), whose powers' focus on sickness and the world's diseases began with the circumstances of his birth. He was born with many sores and was very sick; Nanã abandoned her baby son at the mouth of a cave, close to the beach. There Omolu stayed until Yemanjá found him, washed him in seawater and treated his wounds. From this point on, Yemanjá adopted Omolu as her son.

I like discussing Nanã's approach to motherhood precisely because she refuses to continue being a mother. Juliana Letícia da Silva Oliveira and Isabela Saraiva de Queiroz present an interesting reading of Nanã as a mother in their article 'Motherhood according to Yoruba Mythology: Nanã, Yemanjá, Oxum and Yansã':

> The relationship between Nanã and Omolu may take us back to the stories of women who, for various reasons, experience some suffering and cannot or do not wish to care for children they birth. They highlight a sensitive aspect of motherhood, which is far from being all joy, one that's rarely articulated within families, more widely in the media or even among health professionals, to whom these stories may come as a shock. If for Christians it is a blessing to be a mother and one that Mary never doubts, Nanã shows that joy in motherhood is not a fact or given to all, and that, even so, she is no less revered as an *iabá*.[13]

In *The Second Sex*, Simone de Beauvoir makes an interesting claim about motherhood: 'There is no such thing as an "unnatural mother", since maternal love has nothing natural about it: but precisely because of that, there are bad mothers'.[14] I like to reflect on this assertion which deconstructs the vision responsible for trapping women in a few fixed roles and also makes them feel guilty when they have difficulty with breastfeeding or bringing up their children, for example. It removes the pressure of 'but you should know how to do this; it's in your nature'.

Those who take Nanã Buruku's epistemology as their starting point find comfort for their pain. How many of us blame ourselves for not living up to our expectations of being a 'real mother'. At the same time, de Beauvoir's assertion is liberating in breaking with the idea that all mothers are kind and caring. Yemanjá was mother to many children; Nanã chose not to be. Mothers are people; they are human beings, with all their natural complexities and contradictions.

Oxum

A great witch and *orixá* connected to waterfalls and freshwater bodies, it is to Oxum that the *povos de santo* turn when they are praying for fertility. She is often affectionately referred to as 'Mamãe Oxum' or 'Mama Oxum', and she brings her blessing to all the children who amuse her. There's an *itan* that includes this interesting line: 'before she looks after her children, Oxum polishes her jewellery'. I like to quote this line particularly because the *orixá* is teaching her followers the value of self-care, in a more real sense than as the familiar foolish buzzword, an individualistic principle exclusive to the rich or a kind of lifestyle only for certain classes. For wealthier women, self-care is just a moment of distraction from life's problems, a banality which, as such, is neither interesting nor appropriate for black women, who are obliged to work. This colonial logic has had real consequences in the world of the latter. The women in my family felt its force powerfully and almost never found any time to focus on themselves.

Nonetheless, I do think that Oxum's metaphorical injunction to 'polish your jewellery before looking after your children' invites further adaptation for different perspectives. See, for example, this *itan*, recorded by Verger, in which

MOTHERHOOD FROM A IABÁ POINT OF VIEW

Oxum makes all the women sterile as a way of sabotaging the patriarchal contract:

> When all the *orixás* arrived on the earth, they organised meetings which women were not allowed to join. Oxum was annoyed at being set aside and unable to take part in the discussions. In revenge, she made all the women sterile and blocked all the gods' projects from working out well. In desperation, the *orixás* went to Olodumaré to explain that things were going badly down on Earth, despite the decisions made at their assemblies. Olodumaré asked if Oxum was participating in the meetings and the *orixás* said no. Then Olodumaré explained that without Oxum's presence and her power over fertility, none of their enterprises would be successful. Back on Earth, the *orixás* invited Oxum to join their work, and eventually she accepted, after much entreaty. Then the women became fertile once more and all the projects turned out well.[15]

This *itan* about Oxum cleaning her jewellery is an interesting one to reflect on. It ought to reach all women before they have children. For black women, the silencing is a crucial aspect to consider. As Audre Lorde put it: 'there are so many silences to be broken'. In her essay 'The Transformation of Silence into Language and Action', Lorde makes a provocation:

> What are the words you do not yet have? What do you need to say? What are the tyrannies you swallow day by day and attempt to make your own, until you will sicken and die of them, still in silence? Perhaps for some of you here today, I am the face of one of your fears. Because I am woman, because I am Black, because I am lesbian, because I am myself – a Black woman warrior poet doing my work – come to ask you, are you doing yours?[16]

In the wake of these considerations, I think of Oxum's mothering as a model founded on children's love and protection, but also strongly focused on strategies of infiltration – a watery process – of the patriarchal structures erected for the purpose of women's circumscription.

Conclusion

For me, talking about Candomblé means talking about my childhood, my family, my mother and my grandmother – who was one of Nanã's daughters.[17] It means talking about the female descendants of enslaved people, who landed on the Brazilian littoral, trafficked there by Portuguese, French and Dutch colonisers as well as many other fortune-hunters who made their millions through this vilely dehumanising process and condemned their human 'goods' to misery.

Great creativity was required to develop survival strategies in the teeth of such a powerful enemy. With the *orixás* in these women's hearts, great faith and love by way of religion were required in order to resist the colonisers' impositions. It was also crucial that the people's deep roots remain intact, as a force unifying communities that were otherwise shattered by slavery but could then reunite by way of their deep connections to Africa.

And on thinking about motherhood in the Candomblé communities' cosmogony, we can begin to see the wealth of resonances empowering these women and healing their injured female principles – principles that were only patched together under a dictatorship of submission and on the basis of a compulsory form of motherhood. By contrast, a religion 'gestated' in women's potency within the religious community may forge a fresh powerfulness, or indeed – in Oyá's epistemology – may brew a veritable thunderstorm to strike at the realms of colonial power. I hope that this short text brings

MOTHERHOOD FROM A IABÁ POINT OF VIEW

inspiration to the anglophone women of colonised countries, too, whatever their social backgrounds, encouraging them to reflect and to welcome these new knowledge systems about alternative motherhoods, even in this brief form.

Translated from Portuguese (Brazilian) by Sophie Lewis

Notes

1. Pierre Fatumbi Verger, *Orixás: Os Deuses Iorubás na África e no Novo Mundo* [*Orishas: The Yoruba Gods in Africa and the New World*] (Salvador: Corrupio, 2005).

2. Reginaldo Prandi, *Mitologia dos Orixás* [*Mythology of the Orishas*] (São Paulo: Companhia das Letras, 2000), 382.

3. Carla Akotirene, '*Salve Yemonja! A saúde de nossas cabeças*' ['Hail Yemonja! The Health of our Heads'], in *Vogue*, Brazil, https://vogue.globo.com/Vogue-Gente/noticia/2021/02/salve-yemonja-saude-de-nossas-cabecas.html?fbclid=IwAR3i_HsF8C2ATdcgDdYRbhX_TFyFNZUcYwOhrzgvwG7KNJIld P4A8gGVulM.

4. Djamila Ribeiro, '*No Dia de Iemanjá, minha homenagem à uma estudante*' ['On Yemanjá's Day, My Tribute to a Student'], *Folha de São Paulo*, 2 February 2023, www1.folha.uol.com.br/colunas/djamila-ribeiro/2023/02/flores-para-janaina.shtml.

5. Oyèrónké Oyěwúmí, *The Invention of Women: Making an African Sense of Western Gender Discourses* (Minneapolis: University of Minnesota Press, 1997), 79.

6. Rodney William Eugênio, *A Benção aos mais velhos: Poder e seniori-dade nos Terreiros de Candomblé* [*Blessing to the Elderly: Power and Seniority in Candomblé Terreiros*] (São Paulo: Arole Cultural, 2017).

7. Teresinha Bernardo, '*Candomblé: identidades em mudança*' ['Candomblé: Identities in Flux'], *Revista Nures*, no. 7 (September–December 2007), Pontífica Universidade Católica, 5.

8. Ibid., 6.

9. Geisimara Matos, '*Mãe Pulquéria de Oxossí e a política do carisma*' ['Mother Pulquéria de Oxossí and the Politics of Charisma'], in

Djamila Ribeiro, Maurício Rocha and Lizandra Magon de Almeida (eds), *Uma Nova História, Feita de Histórias: personalidades negras invisibilizadas da História do Brasil* [*A New History, Made of Stories: Black Figures Invisibilised in Brazilian History*] (São Paulo: Jandaíra, 2021), 32.

10. Translator's note: see 'Mangueira 1973 – Lendas do Abaeté', Abre Alas, 30 June 2016, YouTube, www.youtube.com/watch?v=tcCN_ysqboA.

11. Prandi, *Mitologia dos Orixás*, 390.

12. Sueli Carneiro and Cristiane Abdon Cury, '*O Poder feminino no culto aos orixás*' ['Feminine Power in the Worship of the *Orixás*'], in *Escritos de uma vida* [*Writings from a Life*] (São Paulo: Pólen, 2019), 71.

13. Juliana Letícia da Silva Oliveira and Isabela Saraiva de Queiroz, '*Maternidade a partir da mitologia iorubá: Nanã, Iemanjá, Oxum e Iansã*' ['Motherhood according to Yoruba Mythology: Nanã, Yemanjá, Oxum and Yansã'], in *Revista África e Africanidades*, no. 32 (2019): 10, https://africaeafricanidades.com.br/documentos/0270112019.pdf.

14. Simone de Beauvoir, *The Second Sex*, trans. Constance Borde and Sheila Malovany-Chevallier (London: Jonathan Cape, 2009), 644.

15. Verger, *Orixás*, 174.

16. Audre Lorde, 'The Transformation of Silence into Language and Action', in *Sister Outsider: Essays and Speeches* (Trumansburg: Crossing Press, 1984), 41–42.

17. To be called a child of a particular *orixá* indicates a natural affinity with the energies of that *orixá*.

4

Communism's Promise

The Principle of Transnationalism in Feminist and Black Power Organising in the United Kingdom

Lola Olufemi

Crisis is history's black hole

As with all political junctures, radical feminists concerned with the preservation and extension of life find themselves embroiled in the language of crisis. Crisis is a thickened fog that colours how we understand ourselves in relation to the past and future. A consequence of the negative power relations that constitute capitalism, crisis is as Tithi Bhattacharya claims 'an immediate threat generalised to a local community that is played out on a global scale'.[1] This threat is utilised and carefully wielded by liberal democracies whose mandates to govern are forged via a promise to end the latest manufactured threat. The affective consequences of that immediate threat, reaffirmed through discourse, culture and parliamentary politics is the general feeling that we occupy a drawn-out present in which resistance to worsening conditions is futile. The political impasse has swallowed us, we are deadlocked by a two-party system. Gendered violence is ever-present, knitted into the policing and surveillance functions of existence, expressed through cuts to forms of social provision, housing and welfare, in the forced displacement and deadly migration of individuals due to climate catastrophe, notable in the rise of gender fascists' movements across the world who seek to wield state power in order to discipline gender and sex nonconformity out of existence, to banish trans life. We live with knowledge of the frequency of stochastic and material violence committed against us. The language of crisis is purposefully all consuming; the generalised threat appears everywhere at once. It is intended to immobilise us.

One result of the concession to the language of crisis appears in the slow weakening of the core of political consciousness for everyday people: belief in the possibility of transformed material conditions. Whether the crisis is real or imagined, the discursive power of liberal governments enables them to perform an oscillation between crisis and stability, flattening human potential in the process. The linearity of this narrative – periods of crisis give way to periods of stability which inevitably descend into crisis – obscures the exploitative and insidious nature of the profit-motive, turning purposefully lethal relations under capitalism into mere consequences of a failing economy. The oscillation between crisis and stability helps to reassert the disciplinary notion that human life is a chronology of events neatly separated into past, present and future, an ideological premise that is optimal for the suppression of workers. If time is static and progress is stadial, we can only ever move through crisis not around it, we can never reject it outright. Acts of resistance and rebellion break loyalty to temporal regimes by refusing this immobilising orientation. Enacting this break by fortifying a structure of belief capable of withstanding 'crisis' powerfully determines our ability to resist and respond to destruction. A permanent state of crisis serves as a means of reinscribing an order to human life as an 'event' and severs our ability to conceive of a political orientation towards what is not yet known, what cannot yet be conceived but what is necessary to cultivate for the sake of our lives. Operating at more than just a discursive level, 'crisis' and its many shadows intend to break affective attachments to resistance, *to staying alive*, to finding what is habitable amid the most arid conditions. But radical movements, from slave rebellions, to anti-imperialist projects of resistance and localised assaults on agents of the state – police, the army and the bureaucracy – have always depended on the cultivation of an oppositionary state of being.

Bolstered by liberalism's prioritisation of the individual, all manner of crises – political, ecological, bodily, geographical – that refuse to name capitalism as their manufacturer are intended to neutralise political resistance and bolster fascistic relations. Fascism's victory is the ideological manipulation of periods of crisis established by liberal governments which results in a new political reality secured via force. To think alongside Sophie Lewis, if fascism appears as 'a fundamentally colonial matrix of domination, whose cults seek to impose, among other things, right reproduction upon human populations via both positive and negative eugenics',[2] then its purpose is to syphon off and tighten social organisation, to discipline citizens back into the nation-state and to foster myopic and destructive relations. To kill, what Cedric Robinson called, the promise of liberation.[3] Fascism begins with a concession to the language of crisis, when the immediate threat becomes morphological, leaving no space for the creation of new forms of analysis, new conjectures to emerge or ways to historically situate the present. To take COVID-19 as just the latest example of crisis' stultifying force – what has bolstered the ever-present eugenicist logic that drives the engine of capital in this instance is the creation of a consensus that the consequences of the pandemic must simply be accepted, that the 'maintenance of order' in times of exceptional difficulty requires that present conditions remain unchallenged. The

FEMINISM FOR THE WORLD

language of crisis manufactures a political and affective orientation that demands that we look past the precarity of others, that nothing can be done to stop preventable mass death. As Tina Campt writes, care is the antidote, not the treatment, for the wound.[4] As feminists, our duty is, as I have written elsewhere, to break the inertia of this unliveable life.

Crisis is History's black hole. I think alongside Beatriz Nascimento, when she writes that our imperative must be:

> moving past the obstacles put in our way by the perverse visage and oppressive regime of Capital. It was like coming to a conclusion: What use do we have for History? If I am powerless, I have no need of it. History serves those who tell it. Over time, it becomes one with power. In this country, my life is not power, but that is not the end of it... we have not yet been defeated.[5]

We have not yet been defeated. I am reminded that we work inside of the feminist tradition in order to cultivate and reanimate the desire to resist foreclosure. This is a teleology without end. If feminism is one political methodology, one way of conjuring freedom and moving towards it, then it must provide ways of thinking about the present moment that cut across the dichotomy of crisis and stability and in conjunction with other radical political frameworks, produce a challenge to the fascistic forces that constitute History's oppressive character.

Ask for everything

The seduction of meeting the world on its own terms relegates us to the whim of the most reactionary tendencies. To think alongside poet Diane Di Prima, feminists must 'remember, you can have everything you ask for/ask for everything'.[6]

Through an examination of archival material, this chapter explores how the work of Marxist and Anti-imperialist black women and women of colour movements situated in Britain from the 1970s–1990s was underpinned by a core communist principle – transnationalism. Rather than reinscribe them back into the feminist canon, it attempts to trace connections between a range of different groups and individuals that converged using cross-border coalition to enact a break in the manufactured crisis of their lives.

If, as Jodi Dean argues, communism is 'a fact of the world' unspecific to any political history and yet the only political mode of organisation capable of attending to the 'needs, demands and common will of the people',[7] then I begin my analysis with individuals and groups whose provision was labour in service of the will, needs and desires of common people across the world. Engagements with archival ephemera remind us of our collective capacity to reject the terms set by crisis and to understand the 'past' as always already present, intruding in the present moment and determining the temporality of the future. This is communism's promise. If the horizon does not 'await' us, it matters what we do *now* and how we, as feminists, remain attentive to the particularities of our crisis conjuncture.

In exploring the multiple contributions of black and women of colour feminists thinkers and groups situated in Britain and *in* but not *of* that nation – I draw on their practice of transnationalism to argue that they defied the multiple contextual crisis that marked their political lives by an explicit understanding of themselves as related and forcefully attached to others, regardless of geographical location. In thinking across nations and borders but utilising a political analysis that remained attentive to the specificities of geographical localities, these movements remained critical of the bioessentialist mantra of 'global sisterhood', choosing instead to understand their lives as inseparable from the lives of their comrades on the African continent, embroiled in a battle against colonial powers, whose fates were their own. For communist thinkers such as Olive Morris and Claudia Jones, nationhood was anathema to their commitment to the creation of a global critical mass that might provide the ultimate response to capitalist degradation. Joy James' reflection that 'my capacity to love is my capacity to fight'[8] marks the character of their labours: careful strategy, revolutionary love-ethics, armed struggle and confrontation.

The utility of any radical political genealogy is its ability to clarify, to pull into focus the oppressive governing structures that organise social life. Before anything, feminism is a method of analysis, meaning its primary concern is with teasing out the processes, structures and substance of life as we know it in order to move us closer to dignified existence. Feminism offers us not a set of answers, but a means of elucidation. It gives us back the ability to face multiple, overlapping crises via an analysis of the convergent and divergent forces (historical and otherwise) that constitute them. Our only certainty as feminists is that participation in forms of radical organisation is crucial to the improvement of material conditions for all. This remains true especially when the ground beneath our feet begins to shake and our labour, love and perhaps most crucially our time are turned into surplus waste by capital.

One way to resettle our political determination, to refuse the 'end' that crisis imposes and rediscover the connectivity that undergirds resistant desire, is by examining the demands and affective orientations stored in archival material, that survive time's ravishment and constitute the reciprocal legacies to which we belong. In order to cultivate the green and red feminist horizon, the abundance borne from struggle, we must be ready to question the ground on which we stand in order to extricate ourselves from immobility.

COMMUNISM'S PROMISE

We have chosen each other

As women and as feminists, we militantly campaigned on a whole range of issues from health and fertility rights to anti-deportation campaigns; from housing and education issues to policing and anti-SUS laws. We campaigned in solidarity with each other and with those of us still 'at home' struggling for National Liberation – the Irish and Palestinian, Eritreans and Namibians, Chileans and the people of El Salvador.[9]

As Karl Marx and Friedrich Engels write in *The Communist Manifesto*: 'The working man has no country'.[10]

Transnationalism as a political principle requires that its proponents strategise about the acquisition, creation and maintenance of freedom across national borders by foregrounding already-existing connections, linkages and forms of movement. Borders create a matrix in which the flow of capital, which necessitates a flow of bodies, pushes people in and out of respective localities, further severing their connections to each other and the means of production on which their lives depend. To break this gridlock is to claim that one's ability to move should not be dependent on the structure of the economy, that a person's quality of life and the capacity to have their needs met should be severed from the colonial geographies that maintain fictional nation-states. If the chains of exploitation are broken, then that sound must be heard across the world. The development of a transnational political ethic allowed for black and women of colour feminist formations in the UK to develop a political consciousness that worked in tandem with the foremost struggles for independence occurring on the African continent. They understood themselves as part of a diaspora struggling for resources withheld from them through violence. In the landmark feminist text, *Charting the*

63

Journey, the authors note: 'Ours then, is a journey – a geographical, social and political journey from the present to the past, from the past to the future – shifting in time and space as required.'[11] A multi-pronged analysis enabled them to understand the heightened stakes of resistance, to extend solidarity transnationally and develop theories and modes of analysis that prioritised labour expropriation and exploitation across the world. Rethinking geography as a journey constituted by antagonistic and colonial forces rather than a steady fact of life clarified the purpose of political struggle.

One of the greatest failures of liberal historiography is the depiction of black and women of colour feminists formations as the antagonistic underbelly of liberal feminism, rather than an examination of the demands of these movements as radical, autonomous and actively critical of Western hegemony. The core operating principle of these Marxist, anti-imperialist feminist movements was the notion that the lives of all people who live under capitalism are entangled. Indeed, in her essay, 'Age, Race, Class, and Sex: Women Redefining Difference', Audre Lorde, whose anti-imperial consciousness and explicit critique of the 1983 US invasion of Grenada is often underappreciated, writes:

> We have chosen each other
> and the edge of each other's battles the war is the same
> if we lose
> someday women's blood will congeal upon a dead planet
> if we win
> there is no telling
> we seek beyond history
> for a new and more possible meeting.[12]

This poetic ode to transnational solidarity explores the agency inherent to its relational promise. Lorde explicitly links to the horizon beyond history and reflects on the necessity of women's movements to recognise the 'sameness of the war', in other words, the totalising nature of imperialist reality. I linger here in order to sketch out the political context in which Marxist and anti-imperialist feminist movements in the 1970s and 1980s operated and to highlight one of their primary aims: undermining the ubiquity of the nation-state. In a political landscape defined by aggressive neoliberalism, the creation of a national character was at the core of the conservative mission. During this period, the reinforcement of Britain's ideological prominence on the global stage through neocolonial endeavours was coupled with the promotion of individualism for British subjects; summarised in Thatcher's famous retort: 'There is no such thing as society, only the individual and his family.' Race remained a firm marker of differentiation in the creation of the nation's body politic. The British citizen's sense of self was premised on a separation between 'them' (read: white populations) and racialised others. The significance of grassroots political movements that sought to break the border, to find commonality in struggle with other racialised subjects by understanding how processes of exploitation were interdependent, cannot be ignored. Black and women of colour movements understood, as Walter Benjamin pressed, that the state of emergency that they found themselves in *was the rule*.[13]

Gathering to make political demands to the state from the imperial core meant a recognition of how lives in the diaspora were dependent on the forced movement of bodies for capital. What is now commonly termed 'The Windrush generation' in the United Kingdom, a term used to describe the migration from the Caribbean from 1948 to 1971, is not often understood as the movement of racialised workers whose labour was coerced through the promise of abundance in order to re-establish the dominance of the British post-war economy.

Transnationalism, which became transnational solidarity in its application, was an attempt to come to terms with this reality and to denaturalise patterns of production and reproduction under racial capitalism in order to propose new modes of social order able to attend to the scale of its destructive power. Transnational thinking also allows us to think beyond temporal boundaries; it argues that while contending with the force of racial capitalism's destructive power in the past, we can simultaneously begin to map its elimination in the ongoing present and our shared creation of the future.

1.

The political ephemera produced by the Brixton Black Women's Group (BBWG) – a Marxist, anti-imperialist organisation founded in 1973, based in South London – illustrates how the desire to communicate across borders was represented intellectually and politically during this period. The visual aesthetics of the group's newsletter *SPEAK OUT!*, priced at 30 pence and distributed locally, utilised one of its recurring and most familiar symbols, a silhouette of a bust of a black woman at the centre of a geometric globe. This visual demonstrated the group's investment in building a framework that foregrounded black women's political analysis, experience and resistance across the world. Their ambitious political project, which worked against forms of state violence in relation to policing, education and housing in the UK, while solidifying links with independence movements abroad, sought nothing less than the total transformation of multiple spatial geographies. The existence of BBWG acted as a meeting point for organisers who were active in multiple sites of revolutionary struggle in the UK and abroad. In *SPEAK OUT!* the reader about the Brixton Black Women's Group, Gail Lewis (2023) states: 'We were connected to other women's organisations fighting around anti-imperialism; to SWAPO Women, Zanu Women and with women from Ethiopia, Eritrea, with Black American Women's organisations, with Irish women's organisations. To some extent, we were also involved with women organising around Palestine and anti-Zionism'.[14]

It is crucial to read the group's actions and cultural production in light of a key period of movements struggling for decolonisation, what Fanon called in 1961, 'a programme of complete disorder'.[15]

Perhaps most crucially, the BBWG's attempts at political education via the newsletter facilitated the circulation of radical ideas to be discussed and questioned across working-class communities. The production of material was driven by a refusal to restrict information that would enable others to break with the hegemonic structures that shaped their everyday lives. Reading Marx alongside black women's political writing at reading groups and conferences foregrounded an intertextuality that aided the synthesis of radical histories of thought. The BBWG produced at least four issues of the newsletter, complete with ideological summations of their positions, book reviews, poetry and illustrations. Working in the legacy of Claudia Jones, whose revolutionary work extended beyond formal party tracts to poetry, the BBWG refused to privilege specific forms of knowledge, understanding the necessity of a full and rich existence made beautiful by art and made liveable by political organisation. In a 1949 essay, 'An End to the Neglect of the Problems of the Negro Woman!', Jones herself wrote: 'The bourgeoisie is fearful of the militancy of the black woman, and for good reason.'[16] A core feature of the group's attempts at cultivating militancy in pamphlets and newsletters was the deliberate omission of the names of authors from collective statements. This acted as a way to evade surveillance from the state but also enabled group members to linguistically exercise their collectivity. The newsletter represented the multiplicity of feminist concern during this period: articles on various issues range from feminist analysis of material conditions in relation to housing, welfare, education and childcare to calls for solidarity for burgeoning women's movements and resistance against Apartheid and fascistic government regimes.

The BBWG emerged from a Black Power movement which often failed to integrate feminist analysis into its understanding of social relations. Numerous oral histories from key members of the group such as Melba Wilson and Gerlin Bean described their migration from the Black Power movement towards the BBWG as a space where black women's critical analysis could be foregrounded and where the specific convergences of race, gender and capitalist exploitation were analysed. The desire for an autonomous women's organisation grew in tandem with a determination to align themselves with radical struggle across the world, to speak not with a singular voice but *towards* a singular oppressive force that manifested across borders.

An article in Issue 4, published in 1982, documents the complexity of the Chilean women's movement, and the strategies devised by working-class women against bourgeois co-optation. Presumably written by a Chilean comrade for a UK audience, the introduction to the piece states:

The following is an article on the various struggles which Chilean women have been involved in since the CIA-backed overthrow of the Allende (Popular Unity) government in September 1973.

[There] is the need to distinguish between those women's organisations which represent and/or serve the interests of the ruling classes and those which represent the struggle of working women, and therefore contribute to the emancipation of all oppressed and exploited people. In this case, the

> article clearly shows that there is no relationship between the needs of the mass of Chilean women and the bourgeois women's organisations espousing their ruling class interests.[17]

The author goes on to note how Chile's fascist government deprived women of their most basic rights, providing a distinctively Marxist commentary on how the fates of the working class were being decided by bourgeois feminist organisations whose interests served private capital. The style of the report demonstrates the complex mechanisms through which comrades across the border informed one another of their relative struggles. *SPEAK OUT!* contained many reports from grassroots struggles across the world; the newsletter's intention was to extract strategic lessons from specific locations that could be applied globally and used to sharpen critique. If bourgeois feminist groups did not serve Chilean women's working-class interests, then they had to be understood as a threat to all women everywhere, from the diasporic communities in the imperial core to the global proletariat rebuilding their nations in the wake of Independence.

This intention established by BBWG was emulated in the numerous other organisations that followed in its wake brought together by the Organisation of Women of African and Asian Descent (OWAAD) in 1978, an umbrella organisation, which was established by Stella Dadzie, Gail Lewis, Olive Morris, members of the African Students Union UK as well as individuals and collectives involved in anti-racist and feminist campaigning across the UK. The formation of the organisation occurred in tandem with the creation of a women's caucus in The Zanu Women's League, the women's arm of the Zimbabwe African National Union-Patriotic Front in 1977. In the *Heart of the Race: Black Women's Lives in Britain*, the authors remark on how the impetus for autonomous black women's organising spaces in the UK were buoyed by the energy of African Independence. Rejecting the meagre ambitions of certain sects of white liberal mainstream and socialist feminisms who failed to integrate race into their analysis of gender, certain organisations in OWAAD were concerned with the cultivation of revolutionary conditions that would lead to the destruction of the colonial nation-state. Despite their existence inside the imperial core, black and women of colour feminists during this period made conscious efforts to understand their bodies as constituted by schemas of power that extended far beyond their positions as 'women'. They understood their bodies as placed inside a colonial matrix and their freedom as dependent on the freedoms of other oppressed subjects – they sought the creation of a global proletarian body politic. Extending the notion that no person is free until women are free, they eschewed the greater acquisition of rights as sovereign subjects in favour of the total destruction of the restraints placed on them by social, political and economic borders. The purposeful alignment of their movements with revolutionary struggles of independence distinguished their ambitions from unsatisfactory calls for 'equality' or 'equal pay'. The importance of the programmes put forward by socialist leaders on the African continent cannot be understated. Geared towards the full participation of women in social life, these created a blueprint for the transformation of social life.

> We were influenced far more, at the time, by what was happening in the liberation movements in the African continent. There were more examples of Black women who were active in revolutionary struggles in places like Angola, Mozambique, Eritrea, Zimbabwe and Guinea-Bissau... what Somara Machel had to say about women's emancipa-

COMMUNISM'S PROMISE

tion made a lot more sense to us than what Germaine Greer and other middle class white feminists were saying.[18]

Their analysis of gender refused to foreclose the The Zanu-PF call for 'Liberation through Participation', which understood women as full participants in the struggle against colonial rule and helped shape the purpose and function of OWAAD as a space and network to link revolutionary women's organising in the UK, to politically educate members and to give them the skills to understand their positions as workers under capitalism. The first Black Women's National Conference, intended to bring together a wide variety of black women's organising groups to politically organise around issues of healthcare, law and immigration took place in 1979 and was documented by filmmaker Menelik Shabazz. It was followed by the founding of *FOWAAD!*, OWAAD's newsletter intended for the dissemination of information. Surviving ephemera from this period, pamphlets, newsletters and videos and images convey the clarity of vision that sparked black and women of colour's autonomous organising efforts in the UK, despite their eventual collapse. Rather than merely a history of dissent, their interventions represent a critical intervention into discourses of feminism which shifted the terrain from reform towards revolution.

2.

OUTWRITE was a feminist newspaper created by a collective of women (The Feminist News Group) which was active in the UK from 1982–1988. First published on International Women's Day on 8 March 1982, it was intended as an internationalist community newspaper for local distribution. Specifically anti-capitalist and anti-imperialist in its framework, *OUTWRITE* sought to make connections between women's struggles across the globe and was motivated by the erasure of 'Black and Third World Women's' feminist resistance. Its founders were variously situated in different elements of the feminist movement with varying levels of experience in print media.

The newsletter operated under the assumption that there were huge swathes of working-class women without access to information about women's struggle globally. It sought to rectify the spread of liberal misinformation through the production of a cheap, accessible document that could demonstrate the myriad demands made from groups of feminist organisers in their respective geographies in an effort to bolster a global women's movement. In a time of neoliberal crisis ushered in by Thatcherism, *OUTWRITE* encouraged women engaged in militant struggle to submit their thoughts, observations and ideas to the paper, building a small team of grassroots 'reporters' based in the UK who challenged the hierarchical nature of the mainstream news media. Seeking to rectify an absence, its editors were determined to cultivate an internationalist feminism capable of surpassing the border and providing a critical account of the ideological forces that reified feminist critique from Europe and the Americas. The editors were explicit in their intention from the newspaper's conception. In a headline article of Issue 56 from March 1987, they ponder the impact of Western hegemony on perceptions of feminism and the 'women's movement'.

> We need to ask, if in fact, most women are opposed to the broad ideals of feminism – increased social and psychological freedoms of women – or if their resistance is to that particular brand of feminism arising out of the white, middle-class experience in the West, but popularly projected as 'The Women's Movement' by the media and most Western, middle-class feminists themselves. Those studies

which have inquired into the consciousness of poor and Third world women without resorting to Western feminist concepts are quite instructive.[19]

During the paper's almost ten-year run, their intention to highlight the contributions of 'Black and Third World Women' was achieved laterally, through a comradely orientation that was dependent on staunch anti-imperialism. This focus highlighted the necessity of analysis from the so-called Global South in proletarian struggle. The group focused on collective modes of writing that conveyed their general understanding of the connectedness of political struggle. They wrote collectively in order to demonstrate their disdain for hierarchy and to provide space for robust critique that did not prioritise individual opinion. *OUTWRITE* emerged through a rich print-making and zine culture during Margaret Thatcher's conservative governance, partly as a resistant action to laws and policies that strengthened police and surveillance power, which reaffirmed the centrality of the nation-state by expelling 'immigrants' and named feminists, queers and sex workers as deviants. During this period, a number of subversive cultural strategies were employed by artists associated with the BLK Art Group, and those engaged in grassroots struggle in order to produce forms of art, culture and political education that stood counter to the oppressive nature of neoliberal governance. Anger fuelled these cultural ambitions, as well as the availability of local government infrastructure which enabled groups and individuals to fund their projects and secure premises from which to operate. In her essay 'Producing a Feminist Magazine', co-founder of *OUTWRITE* Shaila Shah notes that the producers of *OUTWRITE* met weekly at the Central London Women's Centre and worked with other collectives and groups on the advertising, distribution, scheduling and production of the newspaper.[20]

In laying out a case for an internationalist feminism, the authors focused on similarities in working-class women's conditions across the globe and included updates and developments on socialist women's causes. These reports acted as a means of building momentum and developing an ongoing sense of insurgency: that the growth of a global women's movement could not be stopped and that consciousness was being raised in every area of the world. Shah notes that the group thought extensively about its role in the women's movement – whether or not the newspaper could act as the vehicle to change the direction of the women's movement through an examination of the meagre demands of liberal feminism. Most crucially, what remained central was the group's ongoing belief in the relationship between feminist language and action. Whether or not they understood the importance of *OUTWRITE* as a cultural object imbued with revolutionary potential, their work captured the tenacity of a global women's movement whose demands sought to improve the lives of every person.

Rather than begin with an analysis at the Imperial centre and emanate outwards, various articles in *OUTWRITE* were written from the perspective of those directly engaged in struggle outside of Europe, in order to strengthen the ideological bonds between different causes for the purposes of strategic advancement. Shah notes that articles included 'working women's cooperatives in Zimbabwe... Pacific women protesting against the dumping of nuclear waste, speaking out against Zionism'. In Issue 46, they noted the first conference of the Union of Women's Work Committees, which was held on 27 February 1986, in which 'Speakers from all over the Gaza Strip reasserted in speeches and poems the need to unite, to develop self-reliance as women and to participate more fully and equally in the national and social struggle towards the liberation of Palestine.' They note the union's intention to reach over 1,000 members by 1986, stating 'given the fact that from a handful of members in 1983, membership has now reached 700 and given the enthusiasm of women at the conference, this is sure to happen!'

In a double-page spread on women's participation in the ANC in Issue 41 released in 1985, the author, presumably a writer or reporter for *OUTWRITE*, conducts an interview with a spokesperson for the organisation, where she interrogates the party's reformist tendencies and their commitment to armed struggle.

> Q: The talks with the businessmen and the multinationals, is that assuming that the ANC will gain power by negotiations? Am I wrong that the call for armed struggle is a sort of stepping stone to accelerate diplomatic moves... Why did the ANC meet with businessmen? I can't accept your earlier answer of divide and rule. Given that the ANC bases itself on the Freedom Charter and given the recognition that you are representatives of the people in S.A, you are in a strong position – so why negotiate?[21]

Questions like these demonstrate the revolutionary spirit that animated *OUTWRITE*'s project, the serious consideration of the necessity for principled armed struggle, the hunger for transformation that led them beyond the well-erected borders of the British state. Their continued and consistent calls to support the resistance struggle against Apartheid and other forms of nationalised violence was crucial in demonstrating what feminism should endeavour to concern itself with. A document that captures and locates the ambition of feminist radicality, *OUTWRITE*'s vision was always decisive, always capacious, always pushing its readers to hone their critical orientation to the world.

The Feminist Library, located in Peckham, London, houses an extensive collection of *OUTWRITE* newspapers. For the majority of the newspaper's active years, it was reliant on funding from the Greater London Council for production costs. *OUTWRITE* exists as an important artefact from an era in which working-class communities had not yet been totally abandoned by the state: grassroots organising thrived due to government policies which provided free education, greater availability of council housing and a semblance of social welfare before the onset of the Thatcher years in which these resources were destroyed. The purpose of such funding had long-lasting consequences on the organisational landscape at the time which simply does not exist for feminist organisers today. However, *OUTWRITE*'s inability to source a form of independent funding contributed to its limited reach and eventual disbandment. Shaila Shah writes of the group's many dashed ambitions as a result of ideological divisions among its editorial group and cramped and unsustainable working conditions.

OUTWRITE, as a singular piece of cultural production, might be understood as a prime example of communism's promise, a transnational alliance that fortified the always overlapping resistance struggles intended to upend oppressive conditions. However, Tracy Fisher and a number of other scholars have written about the institutionalisation of many black and women of colour organisations which began as grassroots endeavours during the 1980s, due to an overreliance on government funding to prop up core organising structures.[22] This institutionalisation turned many autonomous organising groups and DIY spaces into service providers, which brought with it deeply conservative ideological shifts. Southall Black Sisters, the domestic violence service provider to which a number of contributors and editors belonged, has come to represent some of the most reactionary elements of liberal feminist politics in the UK, embedded in a deeply carceral and biologically essentialist Violence Against Women Sector. I include this contradiction here in order to note the complexity of the present-day feminist landscape that continues to be haunted by the revolutionary and reactionary elements of radical collectives like *OUTWRITE*.

3.

In Jessica Huntley's archive, I come across a small scrap of paper – the cursive handwriting reads:

The struggle of our people in the Caribbean against the exploitative system generated and perpetuated by international [illegible word] capitalism is our struggle too.[23]

is our struggle too.

This statement is emblematic of the central principle of Huntley's political framework. The reclamation of the struggles of postcolonial nations as 'hers' and therefore 'ours' locates the struggle for freedom as a global project. Though it is unclear whether or not Jessica wrote this note, it seems fitting among her papers as a summation of the driving force behind her political life. Born in so-called British Guiana in 1927, Huntley arrived in the United Kingdom with her husband Eric Huntley, as founding members of the socialist People's Progressive Party in British Guiana in the 1950s. Both became centrally involved in grassroots Black Power struggles against the colour bar, police violence and the advancement of the supplementary school movement. The two are known, perhaps most famously, for the establishment of Bogle-L'Ouverture publishing company in 1969. Rather than firmly assimilate into middle-class life, Jessica Huntley's archive is testament to an infusion of the desire for freedom in her everyday life: through the creation of spaces for individuals to make demands to the state and to raise political consciousness via an interrogation of the neocolonial structures that disciplined black people with violence and trapped them in poverty globally. The revolutionary stature of this work is not often read through a feminist lens, but Huntley understood, as all radical feminists do, the constitutive nature of oppressive forces and the necessity for a response that took into account enduring interdependence.

Always determined to expose the enmeshment of lives under global capitalism, Eric and Jessica were the first to publish Walter Rodney's seminal text, *The Groundings with My Brothers* in 1969. Bogle-L'Ouverture publishing began as a small bookshop operating out of the Huntley's home and then expanded onto commercial properties. Eric and Jessica helped to found the first International Book Fair of Radical Black and Third World Books, using the Bogle-L'Ouverture bookshop, later renamed the Walter Rodney Bookshop, as a meeting space to facilitate the growing Black Power movement in the United Kingdom. Stalwarts of Black British Publishing, they aided the circulation of a number of texts related to black struggle, slavery and anti-colonial rebellion. In the 1983 edition of *The Groundings with My Brothers*, Jessica and Eric Huntley write:

> We... became part of a broader alliance of the Black Parents Movement, Black Youth Movement and the Race Today Collective. It was an alliance which helped form the Committee Against Repression in Guyana and forged the struggles in London and other parts of Europe during 1979/1980, when the working people of Guyana stood firm against the repression of the Burnham Government, eventually leading to... support of Walter Rodney after he was banned from the University of Guyana... At each crucial juncture, we were expected and did in fact rally much needed personal and political support [for Walter Rodney]. With his assassination, we not only mourn the passing of an author but also a friend and comrade.[24]

Despite her location in England, Huntley's archive is littered with countless letters, pleas for support and organisational notes relating to the ongoing battle against repression conducted under Forbes Burham's premiership and the widespread opposition to the removal of Walter Rodney's teaching post at the University of Guyana on the basis of his revolutionary politics. Documentation from the Committee of Concerned West Indians notes multiple actions in solidarity and the clear dissenting voices from the diaspora to Burham's government. One of the group's press releases reads:

> Quite recently, the government bulldozed workers and peasants who occupied the lands of Booker Bros Mcconnell Limited.[25] The government continues to deny freedom of press to the point of imposing control on the importation of newsprint...
>
> To condemn the highhanded action of the Government of Guyana against Guyanese people, we are holding a protest meeting at Conway Hall, Red Lion Square on Friday the 13th September 1974 at 7pm.[26]

Several telegrams document her work as part of the Committee of Concerned West Indians to publicise Walter's ban, including a letter to the Guyana High Commission in 1975 which describes the committee's picketing of the offices of the Guyana High Commission in September of the previous year and the lack of response from the commission despite promises to produce writing that recognised the protest.

A telegram from the editor of the *Times*, dated 25 September 1974 reads:

> Dear Ms Huntley,
>
> While it was not possible to print the letter you kindly sent recently, the Editor assures you that your remarks were read with interest here.[27]

FEMINISM FOR THE WORLD

This trail of correspondence testifies to the veracity of Huntley's Marxism; her organising and campaigning efforts began from the position of peasant workers in British Guiana. Her archive evidences a commitment to naming and therefore denaturalising the oppressive conditions in which she lived. Her focus remained on not only extending solidarity to the poorest in the diaspora but ensuring that the histories of black radical resistance were widely available via education in the United Kingdom. This community-based work, built on gendered labour expressed through a care ethic, is a political practice that remains under theorised outside feminist circles. Given her role in the creation of the first government of British Guiana, Huntley's centrality to radical black political life in the UK is no surprise. It is important to note that her political consciousness formed long before contact with the imperial core; one might read it as a natural consequence of living under colonial rule. Her creation of a plethora of radical texts that registered the descent of West Indian communities in affairs both inside and outside of the United Kingdom demonstrates how the principle of transnationalism frees radical consciousness from the cage that is the border. Radicalism is a free-floating phenomena.

The revolutionary aims of Huntley's work, the expansion of knowledge through radical publishing, the preservation of cultural history and the project of securing freedom for workers could not be contained by geographical location – her ideas and political mobilisations spread widely. The consciousness-raising element of the aforementioned protests organised by Huntley implored working-class people in the diaspora to understand themselves as part of a global class, which required them to take up the grievances and resistance efforts of movements abroad as if they were their own. Huntley stood firmly against the logic of crisis, opposing colonialism's violent separation and dispersals of people: its alienative purpose, its designation of those deserving of life, its ability to fracture and reinscribe individuals into fixed locations. She used the resources at her disposal to denaturalise the power of governmental regimes and to support attempts at grassroots rebellion everywhere. She understood that the history of one nation is the history of all nations and that the task of anyone engaged in struggle is to acknowledge those 'across' the border as co-creators of resistance.

Our affairs and our destiny

In a 'Sister's Trip to China', an account of a student delegation visit organised by the Society for Anglo Chinese Understanding in 1977, published in *SPEAK OUT!*, Olive Morris writes:

All African and Asian people are members of the Third World, with a common history of colonialism and imperialist exploitation. Many of our countries have kicked out their foreign exploiters and some are still doing so, but in many where independence has been achieved we are still not in full control of our affairs and destiny.[28]

In response to the crisis of her life – the struggle of so-called 'Third World' nations to free themselves from the imperialist grips of Euro-America – Olive Morris and other racialised feminists forged bonds of solidarity that would bring them closer to those engaged in struggle through critical analysis and practical action. Here 'solidarity' was not the extension of a hand performed from the centre to the periphery; rather, it was a reciprocal movement that recognised the impossibility of the individual. When Morris speaks of 'our affairs and destiny', she speaks not of the bounded nation that exists always as a potential threat to others but towards communism's promise: collectivised existence, a world where we are all able to be rich in need. The cultivation of a place where the border no longer determines the trajectory of one's life.

Refusing to capitulate, Morris and her comrades responded to crisis with a care ethic that worked against the logic of capital extraction and state abandonment, seeking instead to meld their political visions with those located beyond the places their eyes could see. This solidarity had no conditional limits: rather than form bonds on the basis of their categorical positions as 'women', they instead understood themselves and others as part of a *universally subjected class* (unevenly constituted by race and gender) who could rescue their destiny from the grips of patriarchal, capitalist regimes of power. Whether explicit or not, this gesture demonstrated feminism's greatest methodological strength: to map out the contours of political struggle and refuse to capitulate to the crisis/stability dichotomy on which liberal democracies depend.

In the words of Jacqui Alexander, transnational feminism is:

> A way of thinking about women in similar contexts across the world, in different geographical spaces, rather than as all women across the world; an understanding of a set of unequal relationships among and between peoples; and taking critical antiracist, anticapitalist positions that would make feminist solidarity work possible.[29]

The principle and ethic of transnationalism tests the limits of fixed concepts: it asks us to trespass in order to strengthen a joint rejection of the terms set by nation-states and their governments. What animates the scraps that I have exhumed from the archive and displayed here is a vigorous desire to get beyond the self; to name a common oppressor and to do everything in one's power to ensure the destruction of capital: that life-sucking force that shapes day-to-day existence. This transnational ethic acts as a redirective; against the prevailing misery of the day, it orientates us in another direction, gives us a taste of *that future that could be now, that should be now, that we must make now.* The belief ushered in by transnational solidarities acts as a salve to discourses of crisis that give way to affective and political immobility. Rather than promise solace from dispute or dissent, working across borders demonstrates that it is possible to move: politically, socially, culturally – it reminds us of the power we possess to dismantle and reconstruct a world reliant on mass death and exploitation.

What we stand to learn from the transnationalist tendencies of Black Power and feminist movements is not their unity or conformity but their ability to build the foundations of connectivity: a constant willingness to learn and grow across the border's dividing lines, a circulatory handling of information, skills and resources, and the propensity to draw from the swell of one movement as another appears to recede. Transnational solidarity attempts to clear a path through a destroyed landscape – it reminds us of each other's utility and foregrounds freedom as a place we can rehearse, build, discover, design, make, shape, move towards, strategise about and craft collectively. Its enduring lesson is that freedom is only possible if it is shared.

If crisis haunts us, it is because time is not linear: the 'past' has come back again and brought with it the same duty: resistance. Transnationalism, which pays close attention to how capital accumulation requires the uneven distribution of labour exploitation and imperialist ambitions driven by the profit-motive determine global existence, is a powerful strategic tool. It emphasises that freedom involves a fellowship of others and an opposition to the forces that intend to discipline us into one place, at one time. Engaging in principled struggle together disrupts and destroys the flow of capital: this threat is communism's promise. We must endeavour to keep it.

Notes

1. Tithi Bhattacharya, 'Confronting the Specters of Marxism: Analysing New Currents in Intersectional, Feminist, Queer, and Transgender Marxism in Times of Multiple Crises', keynote address at conference, University of Bielefeld, 13–14 October 2022.

2. Sophie Lewis and Asa Seresin, 'Fascist Feminism: A Dialogue', *TSQ* 9(3) (August 2022): 463–479, https://doi.org/10.1215/23289252-9836120.

3. Cedric Robinson, *Black Marxism: The Making of the Black Radical Tradition* (London: Penguin Classics, 2021).

4. Tina M. Campt, keynote address, 'Loophole of Retreat: Venice', United States Pavilion at Venice Biennale, October 2022, available on YouTube, www.youtube.com/watch?v=91bWInpKlVs.

5. Christen Smith, Archie Davies and Bethânia Gomes, '"In Front of the World": Translating Beatriz Nascimento', *Antipode* 53(1) (2021): 279–316, https://doi.org/10.1111/anti.12690.

6. Diane Di Prima, *Revolutionary Letters* (London: Silver Press, 2021).

7. Jodi Dean, *The Communist Horizon* (London: Verso, 2021).

8. Joy James, keynote address, 'Captive Maternal Contradictions: The Limits of Advocacy when "Black Women Save Democracy"'. Department of Gender Studies, Cambridge University, 25 January 2021. www.gender.cam.ac.uk/Events/genderseminars/seminararchive.

9. Shabnam Grewal, Jackie Kay, Liliane Landor, Gail Lewis and Pratibha Parmar, 'Preface' in Shabnam Grewal, Jackie Kay, Liliane Landor, Gail Lewis and Pratibha Parmar (eds), *Charting the Journey: Writings by Black and Third World Women* (London: Sheba Feminist Publishers, 1988), 2.

COMMUNISM'S PROMISE

10. Karl Marx and Frederich Engels. *The Communist Manifesto* (New York: Oxford University Press, 1992).

11. Grewal et al., *Charting the Journey*, 2.

12. Audre Lorde, *Sister Outsider: Essays and Speeches* (Trumansburg, NY: Crossing Press, 1984).

13. Walter Benjamin, *On the Concept of History* (Createspace Independent Publishing Platform, 2016).

14. Milo Miller (ed.), *Speak Out! The Brixton Black Women's Group* (London: Verso, 2023), 293.

15. Frantz Fanon, Richard Philcox, Homi K. Bhabha, Jean-Paul Sartre and Cornel West, *The Wretched of the Earth*, 60th anniversary edition (New York: Grove Press, 2021).

16. Claudia Jones, 'An End to the Neglect of the Problems of the Negro Woman!' (1949), *PRISM: Political & Rights Issues & Social Movements*, https://stars.library.ucf.edu/prism/467.

17. Miller, *Speak Out!*

18. Beverley Bryan, Stella Dadzie and Suzanne Scafe, *The Heart of the Race: Black Women's Lives in Britain* (London: Virago, 1985), 148–149.

19. *OUTWRITE*, 56, March 1987. Retrieved from Feminist Library.

20. Gail Chester (ed.), *In Other Words: Writing as a Feminist*. Routledge Library Editions Feminist Theory 18 (London: Routledge, 2013).

21. *OUTWRITE*, 41, 1985. Retrieved from Feminist Library.

22. Tracy Fisher, 'Race, Neoliberalism, and "Welfare Reform" in Britain', *Social Justice* 33(3) (105) (2006): 54–65, www.jstor.org/stable/29768385.

23. Jessica Huntley and Eric Huntley, HUNTLEY, ERIC AND JESSICA {GUYANESE BLACK POLITICAL CAMPAIGNERS, COMMUNITY WORKERS AND EDUCATIONALISTS}, LMA/4463, London Metropolitan Archives, 2012.

24. Walter Rodney, *The Groundings with my Brothers* (London: Bogle-L'Ouverture, 1969).

25. Booker Group was the largest manufacturer, retailer and employer in British Guiana. Established in 1870, it began as a company harvesting sugar.

26. Jessica Huntley and Eric Huntley, HUNTLEY, ERIC AND JESSICA.
27. Ibid.
28. Miller, *Speak Out!*
29. Sara Salem, 'Transnational Feminist Solidarity in a Postcolonial World', *The Sociological Review Magazine*, 3 July 2019, https://thesociologicalreview.org/collections/politics-of-representation/transnational-feminist-solidarity-in-a-postcolonial-world/.

5

Truly Radical

Transfeminist Struggles in the Face of the Anti-Gender Neo-Conservative Turn and its Convergence with the Trans-Exclusionary Movement

Sayak Valencia

A little background

I write this text at a very difficult moment for the transfeminist struggle in Mexico. On this day, 21 February 2023, a group of community activists in Mexico City were physically attacked by the city police during a demonstration against the draft law put forward by América Rangel, a deputy for the right-wing PAN party, to prevent young trans people from having the right to decide over their bodies.[1]

Unfortunately, such scenes of physical violence and discrimination against trans communities have become increasingly common ever since the starting pistol was fired by the ascent to power of far-right presidents Donald Trump in the USA and Jair Bolsonaro in Brazil.[2]

This full-on violence against trans communities and other vulnerable communities such as both undocumented and documented and/or racialised migrants around the world does not happen in isolation; it is part of a plot carefully orchestrated by the rejuvenated far right, which is seeing new adherents worldwide.

As Daniel Kent Carrasco and Diego Bautista Páez asserted in 2020 in *Revista Común*, the ideological enthusiasm for the far right has expanded across the Atlantic with the resurgence of:

> [N]eonazis in Greece, Germany and Ukraine; Francoists in Spain; white supremacists in the United States and the United Kingdom; and xenophobic regionalists in England, Italy, France and Scandinavia. [But also] on the streets of the Third World, fuelling the origins of the farcical obscurantism of Bolsonarism in Brazil, the consolidation of the openly fascist agenda of the transnational Hindu Right, the conservative Turkish ethno-nationalism led by Recep Tayyip Erdoğan, the genocidal gangsterism of Rodrigo Duterte's government in the Philippines, the ultra-securitarian regime of Nayib Bukele [in El Salvador] and the resurgence of the reactionary, classist, Catholic and racist ultra-right in Mexico.[3]

This authoritarian right wing, with its mostly (though not exclusively[4]) neoliberal bent, continues to manage the markets and as a result has enough capital at its disposal to take over digital platforms and adopt controversial public figures to spread its reactionary and anti-rights messages both virtually on social networks and in the physical spaces of academia, culture (in all its facets) and different kinds of activism.

One of the most notorious strategies of this expansion of conservatism is the reappropriation of critical theories to fill them with ultra-conservative content that once again positions the authoritarian state as an ideal, reflecting a theory of value that favours the traditional family, religious values, and a defence of extreme nationalism and nativism. On top of this,

TRULY RADICAL

they make a continual appeal to binary, essentialist arguments that postulate biological sex as inalienable and inarguable.

In this type of discourse, three types of 'charismatic' figures emerge that at first glance seem to pertain to different symbolic orders but in fact converge in a neo-fascist dystopia:

1. Provocative and openly misogynous cis men, mostly but not always heterosexual. I think it is important to point this out because while it is true that the values defended by conservative agendas are semiotically embodied in cisgender, heterosexual bodies, this is not universally the case. We must remember that this far-right agenda loves to mix up critical discourse with reactionary content, as well as co-opting or creating controversial figures or influencers who come from oppressed groups or opposed to the conservative agenda, precisely to undermine the struggles and demands for rights of these people. For example, the alt-right Trump administration strengthened its presence online through incendiary posts with politically incorrect, openly misogynist, racist and xenophobic content published by figures such as Milo Yiannopoulos,[5] a perfect example of these dissonant icons who downgrade certain identities – gay in this case – to undermine the legitimate claims of communities such as the LGBTQ+ community.

2. Heterosexual cis women who present themselves as influencers of various kinds and who actively reproduce the gendered choreographies of femininity. Whether it be embodying the perfect mothers, wives, daughters and/or as businesswomen who believe in economic empowerment of women and their integration into global markets, but without challenging the established gender order where the patriarchy and cis-heterosexual, conservative masculinity retain the central position.

Alternately, they may present a commercial aesthetic where, by means of the hyper-sexualised exhibition of their bodies, they respond to the mandate to become entrepreneurs of themselves, generating a bio-hyper-mediated subjectivity that combines material elements of the body with virtual prostheses such as facial and body filters that alter their image and propagate the desire for bodily modification among women. The aim is to establish a similitude and verisimilitude between the biopolitical ideals of gender, sexuality and class under neoliberalism, through a body that is transformed into a kind of fleshy screen. In this way, they disseminate a new model of gendered domesticity that brings together the logics of advertising, surveillance, gender binarism, obligatory cis-heterosexuality and racist, sexist, aporophobic politics; logics spread via embellished images and that reproduce conservative ideals or dilute the need to politicise our situations of structural and structuring inequality.

3. Trans-exclusionary feminists, who through their transphobic and anti-rights activism abandon the agenda of equality and social justice to shift perilously close to the discourses spread by ultra-conservative agendas, even in some cases signing up to anti-abortion positions. For example, in Mexico the lesbian writer Laura Lecuona recently claimed, at the presentation of her anti-trans rights book, that to halt the trans movement she was prepared to make pacts with the Mexican right and its anti-abortion agenda. This contravenes one of the pillars of the feminist agenda: the right to decide over one's own body, in view of which free and legal abortion has historically been defended by all feminist movements regardless of their differences.

In this repressive, moralising context, attacks on the trans communities in Mexico have become more and more widespread,[6] as well as others that declare themselves to be progressive, such as Spain, the scene of lamentable examples of the intersection between anti-gender policies, racism and coloniality. Spanish philosopher Amelia Valcárcel, for example, never misses an opportunity to attack trans people and the queer movement as if they were the same thing. Among other things, she demonstrates a total lack of understanding of the themes and real agendas of these groups, encouraging disinformation.

Valcárcel distorts and trivialises the objectives of the programme for equal rights for all people that is historically supposed to be defended by self-proclaimed 'equality feminism', for which she has campaigned unceasingly in recent decades without ever relinquishing her colonial and discursive power over other non-white feminists, refusing to accept that feminism can have genealogies other than that of the European suffragist path.

She does so by broadcasting her messages on reactionary religious and far-right media such as COPE radio,[7] which under Franco's dictatorship was a fascist political and religious propaganda organ – as it remains today. And she is not alone in forging alliances with the far right by creating discursive and political oxymorons.

Other distressing and dangerous examples of the fascist drift that seeks to usurp the anti-dogmatic and libertarian ideals of feminisms have emerged in force in the UK with lesbian separatist theorists like Sheila Jeffreys or anti-trans rights campaigner Lisa Morgan, who misguidedly quoted *Mein Kampf* at a public rally organised by another trans-exclusionary campaigner, Kellie-Jay Keen-Minshull, better known as Posie Parker, in January 2023.[8] The video was posted on Twitter, sparking a digital battle astonishing for the fervour of the belligerents on both sides.

These examples are just a small sample of this terrifying return to the most conservative values on family and sexuality, and to the idea of the strong, macho nation-state, where political value theory is transformed into visceral diatribes, personal attacks and colonial outbursts rather than giving way to a genuine Realpolitik.

Several books and surveys on the subject, such as *La reacción patriarcal. Neoliberalismo autoritario, politiћación religiosa y nuevas derechas* [*The Patriarchal Backlash: Authoritarian Neoliberalism, Religious Politicisation and the New Far Right*], edited by Marta Cabezas Fernández and Cristina Vega Solís in 2022, attest to the link between the rise of hate speech against trans and transfeminist communities by trans-exclusionary feminisms and their rapprochement with the wealthy far right.

It is therefore impossible not to see the contradictions inherent in this 'trans-exclusionary equality feminism'. This regressive splitting of feminisms as a result of the polarisation generated by groups of so-called anti-trans and trans-exclusionary feminists (generally white and from academic, political and cultural spheres of power, but also from colonial territories) is very worrying for several reasons:

1. Because the emancipatory project of feminisms cannot belong to any given group.

2. Because activism as part of an exclusive movement that incites social hatred and symbolic, economic, political and physical violence cannot be seen as liberating.

3. Because the use of the word 'radical' out of context serves to de-historicise the feminist movement. Furthermore, as we will see, using the word to polarise and not to attack the root of problems gives succour to those who undermine the rule of law to infuse our political agendas with a kind of 'regressive sensibility',[9] while this fragmentation of movements nourishes the conservative political project.

Truly Radical

4. Because their argument, based on an appeal to biology yet with a profound ignorance of biomolecular biology, reduces this discipline to reactionary slogans that instil hatred and accommodate the ideas of sexual binarism proposed by cultural essentialism without a truly scientific basis. And, on the other hand, appealing to scientific legitimacy as unquestionable and produced ex nihilo, while evading its power relations with cis-heteropatriarchy, is an oxymoron for the feminist movement itself, since, as feminist and new materialist epistemologies have shown, Western science has historically constructed the female subject as subaltern and rationally inferior.[10]

A little history... on the true meaning of the term 'radical' and its connection with feminism

In this section, I will briefly analyse the etymological meaning of the word 'radical' and its connections with certain agendas in radical, separatist, lesbian and non-white feminism, above all in the United States. I will also examine the extractivist, distorted and dogmatic way it is used by trans-exclusionary feminisms, which claim it as their own, de-historicising it and turning it into a pastiche of ideas incompatible with anti-dogmatism as the foundation of feminism. 'Radical' in the contemporary context is understood to mean 'polarised', in a discursive montage that produces a kind of cognitive dissonance in the mind of anyone who recalls the history of the feminist and separatist movement.

The word 'radical' comes from the Latin *radix, radicem*, meaning 'root'. In its very etymology, the word tells us that it has to do with going to the root of things. In the social sphere, 'radical' means engaging in a thorough questioning of the foundations of oppression, and therefore to not be radical means being superficial, complicit with inequalities.

Nevertheless, there remains a dispute over its meaning and a constant distortion of its use.

While in politics the term is used disparagingly, as a synonym for extremism, trans-exclusionary feminisms have distorted its meaning to use it in a manipulative manner to maintain the status quo of *mujerista* feminists who reduce the feminist project to the genitality of cis women. The entire political project of the struggles for social justice of feminised persons, or what they call biological sex as the sole subject of feminism, rests on this corporeal reduction.

However, the appeal to the biological sex of women as the only subject of feminisms is a contradiction in terms, given that it is this biologicist reading proposed by the patriarchy, by way of scientific explanations, that has constructed feminised people with the capacity to bear children as historically and biologically inferior. Thus, being a radical feminist is not compatible with promoting hatred and the exclusion of trans people's rights.

The following is a brief history of the historical and political use of the word 'radical' in conjunction with feminism. As we know, the emergence of radical feminism took place in the late 1960s in the United States of America. Radical feminism emerged from a split in the Women's Liberation Movement (WLM). Considering that both the National Organization for Women (NOW) founded by Betty Friedan in 1966, and the WLM, also founded in the 1960s, were reformist and did not go to the root of the issues raised by critique of the patriarchy, the radicals sought a libertarian revolution for women in all spheres of life, not just traditional issues of political inclusion and equal pay.

However, it is important to emphasise that radical feminism emerged in a context of profound social interrogation, involving organisations that demanded civil rights for populations such as the African-American (Black Power) and Chicano

TRULY RADICAL

communities, as well as pacifist, anti-colonial and New Left movements in the United States, and that many of its members came from diverse militancy backgrounds and belonged to racialised groups and/or identified as lesbians.

These clarifications are necessary to demystify the idea that radical feminism was only white and heterosexual, as stated by Shulamith Firestone in her historical reconstruction of the radical movement, in which she makes important historical oversights and proposes as its icons white feminists with a demonstrable racist history, a fact already criticised at the time by the African-American philosopher Angela Davis in her wonderful 1981 book *Women, Race and Class*.[11] It is also important to understand that some organisational strategies and political decisions carried out by this group of feminists, such as separatism, were inspired by the political organisation known as the Black Panther Party. They considered these strategies necessary because they realised it was not possible to liberate themselves within a cis-male-led left.

Thus, the attempt at radical separation from the patriarchy and its rejection of cis-heterosexual masculinity as the centre of power and oppression has been taken as one of the bastions for 'essentialising' this branch of feminism. Interestingly, this radical split from cis men and repudiation of heterosexuality is no longer treated as a founding slogan today by self-styled RadFem trans-exclusionary feminists, any more than the anti-capitalism that was openly professed by radical feminists in the past.

Another paradox is that although the radicals fought to construct an imaginary for women as an 'oppressed class' and for the elimination of sexual roles, they had to struggle with an underlying contradiction that is repeating itself today:

they promoted the creation of the subject 'woman' or 'women' – which would end up shaping the coherent collec-

95

FEMINISM FOR THE WORLD

tive identity of the emerging movement – at the same time as, paradoxically, they sought to overcome this category. In affirming this intention, they affirmed the certainty that sex was a criterion of political identification. At the same time, however, through the Self-Awareness Groups they tried to make women aware of another certainty, namely, that one is not born a woman, but becomes one.[12]

In a contemporary context where violence of all kinds – sexual, economic, political, but above all physical (of low or high intensity) – is perpetrated on a daily basis against feminised people, it is perfectly understandable that the promise of a community of meaning, belonging and security captures the attention of many women. The open contempt of the authorities fosters mistrust in the institutions of justice and creates social fragmentation, which among many women, especially young women, leads to a state of vulnerability. This enables them to be seduced by the ideas of a radical feminism, misunderstood as trans-exclusionary.

However, the current use of the term by certain transphobic theorists and activists does not adopt the political objectives originally attributed to it. Instead, it gives way to a kind of discursive montage in which playing on the fear of being hurt, discursive tutelage (based on historical ignorance, for some, or the deliberate omission of genuinely libertarian proposals that are incompatible with trans-exclusionary discourse) and incitement to hatred against trans women seem to be the central objectives of the contemporary radical feminist movement. In so doing, these theorists appropriate a vast movement with great internal diversity, and seek to present it solely in opposition to trans women, omitting any mention of 'the realities of trans men who might expose the inconsistencies of their biology-based argument',[13] whereas, as we have seen, while the aims of radical feminists were indeed separatist, they were not necessarily thereby transphobic or trans-exclusionary.

We therefore have to ask ourselves about what kinds of distortion are used to void the movement of its content and instead use it as a Trojan horse to introduce and strengthen conservative agendas that, in the face of *feminist sensibility*, establish a *regressive sensibility* disguised as essentialist indignation.

A brief account of queer theory and its relationship with gender critical theory

One of the rhetorical strategies of trans-exclusionary feminism is its twisting of arguments and appropriation of concepts produced by critical discourse (a strategy it shares with the alt-right). One example is the concept of *gender critical* that was first introduced by queer theory, notably in the 1990s writings of US philosopher Judith Butler in her emblematic book *Gender Trouble*. The problem is that it means precisely the opposite to what trans-exclusionary feminists claim when they call themselves 'gender critical feminists'. Being gender critical represents a paradigmatic shift in de-essentialising the triad sex = gender = heterosexuality, radically questioning the cis-heterosexual and binary perspective on the sex-gender system.

Thus, the queer perspective dismantles the idea of sexual dimorphism as something natural and heterosexuality as obligatory. As Carmen Romero Bachiller says, 'when Butler points out in *Gender Trouble* that "sex was always already gender" she shows that biology is a discourse traversed by genderised expectations and by gender norms: not a neutral discourse at all.'[14]

In this regard, it is important to emphasise that queer theory is not just a discourse but is rooted in social movements and takes up the interrogative mantle of Black, Chicano, lesbian, working-class, radical and other feminisms with regard to the narrow political subject of the white, heterosexual and reformist feminism of the 1960s, embodied by the idea of the Woman without qualifications or intersections.[15]

For this reason, we must note that self-proclaimed 'gender critical' feminists fail to acknowledge the queer genealogy of the radical and critical notion of gender. In doing so, they incur a significant contradiction, as Spanish anthropologist Nuria Alabao has pointed out:

They claim to want to dissolve gender, but question anything that supposedly threatens female identity, such as trans or non-binary identities. They say that if they are free to self-identify – without a mechanism of control, which is currently a medical mechanism – the state's capacity to intervene would be called into question, since destabilising the category of 'woman' jeopardises affirmative action policies or for the protection of women – who are always understood as victims. [...] They claim to fight against gender, yet they reaffirm it by making it the mainspring of their demands for insertion in state policies.[16]

In addition to these contradictions, it is dangerous for feminisms in general to settle on the figure of the victim as the only site of enunciation for feminised bodies; as we know, the alliance between femininity and victimhood has a lengthy history, one that was shaped by the victimisers to taxidermise our demands and to curb our powers of transformation and our political actions.

It is also worth asking why these 'gender critical feminisms' fail to pronounce on subjects such as racial injustice, poverty, nor migratory status or functional diversity as intersections of enormous importance when it comes to considering the life of women today.

Analysing this, we might say that in a context of intensive necropolitics,[17] targeting feminised bodies, cis women's demands for protection from the state voiced through the political lobby of institutional feminism together with 'radical feminists' make no sense, given that the deaths of cis, trans and non-binary women benefit the capital that the state itself administers.

Demanding protection and engaging in dialogue with the sovereign power without questioning capitalism as a necropolitical project that underpins the widespread pillaging on which the contemporary state is based is not feminism but its neoliberal retranslation into the very gender politics it claims to oppose. These represent on the whole the interests of cisgender, heterosexual, white middle- or upper-class educated women who reproduce and seek to ascribe to the sexual rationality of the West. This self-evidently does not involve an iota of radicalism.

Another basic strategy of trans-exclusionary feminism is the use of social networks to propagate its ideas through posts that alter reality, disinform and appeal to readers' emotions, incendiary Tweets and distorted images that present the trans community as an ever-present threat to feminism. With this appeal to the emotions, they seek to establish a shared common sense rather than engage in a dialogue or an in-depth discussion.

In this way, the goal is to conquer[18] people's sensibility, understood as we know it to be 'the faculty of exchanging meaning without using words, the condition of empathic understanding. This faculty is what gives shape to everyday life and ensures mutual understanding within a community'.[19]

Of course, this assault on the emotions by means of digital psychopathology is something that is practised on all sides, left, right and centre. The key to this strategy – and it makes an enormous difference – lies in who possesses the perfect algorithm and the capital to finance their campaign to make these tools more effective.

Transfeminisms and 'mani-fiesta-actions' against necropolitics and the neo-conservative onslaught

I shall now set out a brief genealogy of the links between queer theory and transfeminisms. Broadly speaking, the word 'transfeminism' refers to collectives and groups, both organised and otherwise, that are traversed by processes of mobility between genders and sexualities, but also between territories. In other words, for part of the transfeminist movement, it is not just a question of gender identity politics or of including trans people in feminism, but also of broadening the political subject of feminism (as proposed by various feminist theories, including the queer/cuir perspective),[20] which is no longer conceived solely within the framework of gender binarism nor as a reduction to the corporeality of cissexual women. I'll develop this point below.

The term 'transfeminism' has different meanings and more than one genealogy. In the US context, the coining of the term is attributed to Diana Courvant, who used it for the first time during an event at Yale University in 1992. She and Emi Koyama later launched a website named transfeminism.org, created to promote the Transfeminism Anthology Project, the aim of which was to introduce the term to academia, as well as to locate and connect people who were working on this or similar themes, in order to publish an anthology on the subject.

It was also used by Robert Hill in 2002, who defined it as the incorporation of transgender discourse to feminist discourse. However, the transfeminism we are talking about here is really that which emerged after 2008 through transnational feminist networks, mostly though not exclusively located in Spain, since it is permeated by the practice and discourse of migrant voices and corporealities expressed in study days, seminars, colloquia, demonstrations, etc., which have been held continuously since 2008 in various Spanish-speaking countries, including Mexico.

As an epistemological tool, transfeminism does not dissociate itself from feminism, nor does it present itself as an overcoming of it, but rather as a network capable of opening up spaces and discursive fields to all those practices and subjects of contemporaneity and of *minority becoming* that had not been directly taken into account by white, institutional feminism. In the same way, it forges links with historical memory and acknowledges the legacy of feminist movements that have included racial, sexual, economic and migrant minorities, while at the same time drawing discursively and politically on these same movements. From this perspective, we can trace four intersectional lines in the genealogy of transfeminism:

1. Non-white feminisms of the Third World and the United States Third World.

2. Sexual dissidence and its geopolitical and epistemic displacements to the Global South: from *queer* to *cuir*.

3. The movement to de-pathologise trans identities (*Stop Trans Pathologisation*) and the pro-whore movement, which promotes destigmatisation and legalisation of sex work as well as defusing the insult 'whore', which is used as a weapon hurled at feminised persons who make uninhibited use of their bodies and sexuality.

4. Minority becomings produced by functional diversity, migrations and economic impoverishment.

In these transversal contexts, transfeminisms make a call to propose theoretical-practical updates to reality and the condition of women within it. However, this call is not limited to bodies legible as cis women but includes different corporealities and critical dissidences, being an indispensable requirement that these take into account the specific economic circumstances of the subjects within the international precariat (both economic and existential).

The subjects of transfeminism may be understood as a kind of *queer/cuir multitude* that, through the performative materialisation of the variations of gender and sexuality, succeed in unfolding g-local agency. The task of these *queer/cuir multitudes* is to develop categories and engage in practices that avoid assimilation with the systems of representation imposed by the capitalist hegemony of the heteropatriarchal/classist/racist system. In addition, to invent other forms of action that reconfigure the South as a critical positioning and not only a geopolitical location.

Within this framework, transfeminism is not limited to the incorporation of trans discourse into feminism, but may be understood as a migrant, relational movement, as well as a disobedient counter to the dominant systems of representation and repression, including a direct critique of the dogmatism professed by a certain sector of institutional and/or biologicist feminism.

This confrontation with the homogenising dogmatism of bodies, emotions and desires arises through a reformulation of representations and the entry into circulation of other taxonomies for naming the world.

This, together with the creation of dissident politics of visual attraction that give visibility to *trans-marika-puta-bollo-mestizx-migrante-precarix* movements,[21] while also denouncing the real consequences of the grotesque violence –

fed by machismo, authoritarianism, classism and homophobia – connected with gore capitalism.[22]

Transfeminism takes on its full meaning in a context where capitalism, while remaining an economic system, has diversified to the point of establishing itself as a biointegrated cultural construction, in which the maintenance of the biopolitical and psychopolitical regime is fundamental to the neoliberalisation of the contemporary world.

This neoliberalisation, which was also felt by feminism, works to produce the 'demobilisation of the scenarios of struggle'.[23] For present-day neoliberalism, the production of a 'capitalistic subjectivity'[24] is as profitable as oil and gas, and in it the violence against civilian populations (especially those that present intersections that contravene the mandates of sexual binarism, race, gender, class or functional diversity) also becomes a tool of economic, social, cultural and political control as a result of the deliberate use of massacres in the 'southernised' contexts of the Global North, and in the geopolitical South.

It is for this reason that it is so urgent to situate ourselves, from these different feminisms, as a common front, since as Audre Lorde said in the 1980s, 'without community there is no liberation'; even more, without community there is only a 'temporary armistice between an individual and her oppression'.[25]

In this respect, it is necessary to take up once more the project of creating a common good, one that takes into account that 'community must not mean a shedding of our differences, nor the pathetic pretence that these differences do not exist'.[26] On the contrary, the creation of a common good is based on a self-critical attitude of redefinition that puts on the table the different themes that concerned the first feminisms (equality of rights and access to citizenship), as well as the new feminisms (everyday sexism, femicide, sexual harassment and online violence, multimodal violence) and transfeminisms (destigmatisation of sex work, depathologisation of trans bodies, expansion of the political subject of feminism, intersectionality, colonialism, systemic violence, extractivism, *buen vivir*, etc.) that are ascribed to the specific context of our contemporary realities in the quest for social justice for the majority, and not in a comfortable collusion with anti-rights movements that borders on fascism.

The call made by transfeminisms is for a self-criticism that does not exclude, as subjects of feminism, 'those of us who stand outside the circle of this society's definition of acceptable women; those of us who have been forged in the crucibles of difference – those of us who are poor, who are lesbians, who are Black, who are older',[27] who come from indigenous communities, who are trans, who do not correspond to the Western aesthetic canon, who present functional diversity, who are refugees, migrants, undocumented, precarious, who speak in tongues[28] and who, through their very subjectivising and desubjectivising intersections, suffer the physical, psychological and media-based consequences of the increasing globalisation of explicit, bloody, morbid violence – gore violence, in other words – which has real effects on bodies, usually feminised.

Transfeminism, more than a mere dissident gesture or adoption of a certain aesthetics and prosthetics related to gender performances, appeals to the construction of a common social and political front to account for the violence that artificially establishes and naturalises a 'deliberately fractured narrative strategy'[29] that affects all discursive fields and can be found, in a particularly relentless form, in the way the media present macho violence. Transfeminism as a political front positions itself in 'defence of anti-normative and anti-assimilationist practices and experiences'.[30]

TRULY RADICAL

As a transfeminist, I am not suggesting that the categories that underpin our different intersections and their relation with violence are valid and identical in all contexts and for all feminisms. I understand that violence as a tool of enrichment is expanding more and more to spaces that are geopolitically remote from each other, and that its consequences repeatedly fall on feminised bodies and subjects. Acknowledging this allows us to identify the political cartographies of gore capitalism, given that this violence interweaves with the creation of a subjectivity and an agency determined by capitalism's forces of control and production.

It is from transfeminisms too that we call for a more complex approach to the political subject of feminisms, since we do not seek to reduce the subjects of our struggles. On the contrary, women as the political subject of feminisms exceed the biological essentialism that is proclaimed by trans-exclusionary feminism.

As the political subject of feminisms, women form a critical discursive enclave for understanding that artificial differentiation and naturalisation of inequality on the basis of the binary-sexed body forms part of a project of plunder that begins with the seizure of common property from European peasant populations, the intensive femicide known as the 'witch-hunts', the colonisation of America beginning in the fifteenth century (and the gender coloniality anchored to the coloniality of power, being and knowledge), and crystallising over the seventeenth and nineteenth centuries in a necropolitical process disguised as biopolitics to govern free bodies in America, Europe, Asia and Africa, and inventing political fictions of antagonistic genders, races and sexualities to prevent potential alliances among vulnerable multitudes.

This brief historical recap is intended to remind us that we women, as political subjects and not as sexed bodies, remember our experience of political violence throughout

Feminism for the World

history alongside all those subjects conceived as subaltern or dissident from the point of view of heteropatriarchal and cis-sexual categories.

Different forms of violence (physical, symbolic, economic, psychological, media-based) have been used against us as a kind of pedagogy of subalternisation applied to racialised, poor, feminised or non-binary bodies. These accumulated violences have become a part of our everyday lives, our education, and have had different objectives depending on the historical, geopolitical and economic context in which they are exercised.

The radicalisation of violence situates us on the brink, in the transmutation of an era that demands that we rethink our classical concepts, that we shake up theories to bring them up to date. Indeed, I can echo Barbara Cameron's words: 'I'm not interested in pursuing a society that uses analysis, research, and experimentation to concretise their vision of cruel destinies [...] a society with arrogance rising, moon in oppression, and sun in destruction.'[31] And, above all, I have no wish to reproduce the violence and exclusion of other bodies through trans-exclusionary arguments, which belong to a one-dimensional, simplistic mode of argumentation that resorts to biology as a form of certification and validation of differences, and in doing so encounters its own limits because these are well known as arguments used by the patriarchy to exclude women. Cis-sexist arguments are indistinguishable from racist arguments, since in both cases, the essentialisation and legitimisation of certain bodies – white in the first case, cisgender in the second – makes it possible to conceal and justify the supremacy of one subject over others.

The squabble over representation that raises one identity above others proves to be unrealistic insofar as the ferocity of gore capitalism leaves no other alternatives than the creation of new political subjects for feminism. In other words, 'a becoming woman' understood as 'a rupture with society's current mode of functioning', which forges alliances with other minority becomings and proposes responses to 'a phallocratic mode of production of subjectivity [...] whose sole axis of orientation is capital accumulation',[32] and to which bloody capitalism and cis-masculinity are linked as the cornerstones of the West's political, sexual, racial and economic rationality, deployed in its geopolitics and extended, via the patriarchal connection,[33] to the territories of former colonies.

More specifically, the transfeminist movement seeks to make clear that masculinity (as a living political fiction and not a biological body) is a mechanism for the implementation and conservation of a project of modernity/coloniality and nation that, in its transformation, is linked to the emergence and updating of the capitalist economy. Thus, masculinity as a political fiction is a social phenomenon affiliated to paid work, violence and oppression as ways of giving continuity to projects of social and economic hegemony, overlapping the necropolitical and the biopolitical regime through the Enlightenment model of democracy and the 'heterosexual nation'.[34] The result is that considering oneself a feminist while maintaining a trans-exclusionary position is to make pacts with a necro-patriarchal, pimping, femicidal state that reappropriates our struggles through separatism and the destruction of the common good.

From the transfeminist perspective, we question whether the essentialist genderism that speaks only through and for women who don't want to appear 'aggressive' and accept how 'upsetting' they can be to men (while asking that the 'punishments' for heterosexual, white, middle-class, First-World women, or wealthy Third-World women, not be so exemplary), is not in fact a way of controlling our energies and keeping us occupied with a dialogue that, instead of broadening the political subject of feminisms, obtusely reduces and restricts it.

Finally, this anti-trans becoming by a part of the trans-exclusionary feminist movement is the result of the capture of critical language and its attempt to institutionalise and twist the language of protest. Genderism is a reformist, essentialist movement that at bottom fights for the budgets intended to finance other movements, including those for trans rights, and above all stubbornly refuses to recognise that the rights of trans people are not privileges, and that the acquisition of rights by some populations is never to the detriment of others.

As a neoliberal, neoconservative movement, the trans-exclusionary feminism is ready to identify the consequences of patriarchal or fratriarchal violence but not the root of the problem. That is to say, it is a feminism that does not free itself from the idea of power, but reproduces the pragmatic and rational programme of the West, currently expressed in unbridled neoliberalism, omitting the fact that it is precisely this instrumental reason that underpins the problem of domination and violence of the cis-heterocentric, patriarchal and colonial system, and that it is the intersection of oppressions that enables the system to deploy and fill its coffers – both economic and symbolic – everywhere.

Yet, it is not all bad news, because – despite the prevailing neoliberal necropolitics and the anti-gender and neoconserva-tive assault by transphobic feminists – in Latin America, the non-exclusionary feminist and transfeminist communities (in the broad sense, not only of trans people) are reinventing the political imagination through their practices of denunciation, demands for justice and the construction of agendas in an alliance for the common good.

I call these practices *mani-fiesta-actions* as a kind of reinven-tion of the traditional concept of the political demonstration (*manifestación* in Spanish). This type of practice is characterised by the occupation of public space, playful intervention and refusing to mythologise the figure of 'the victim' as the only rightful posture to take at protests. In this sense, these political imaginaries place the following question at their heart: can you enjoy life while you are in pain?[35]

This question is key to understanding the new transfeminist leaderships and activisms around protest against femicide and transfemicide. The political imaginary of contemporary feminisms makes the equation of the demand for justice more complex, and shows us how people who have survived the femicide or transfemicide of a loved one have become activists, creating new leaderships and redefining the political subject of feminisms not in an essentialist way, but through alliance, the foundation of affective communities, and also by generating a wave of collective and intersectional indignation that refuses to pass through the circuits of victimisation proposed both by trans-exclusionary and essentialist feminisms and by state institutions as the only mode of attention and without reparation of any kind.

Translated from Spanish (Mexican) by Fionn Petch

Notes

1. Daniel Alonso Viña, '*Una protesta por los derechos de las personas trans enfrenta a las autoridades con los manifestantes en el Congreso de Ciudad de México*' ['A Transgender Rights Protest Clashes with Authorities at the Congress of Mexico City'], *El País*, 22 February 2023, https://elpais.com/mexico/2023-02-22/una-protesta-por-los-derechos-de-las-personas-trans-enfrenta-a-las-autori-dades-con-los-manifestantes-en-el-congreso-de-ciudad-de-mexico.html.
2. Even though the problem of fascism 2.0 has very clear antecedents in certain *coups d'état* pre-prepared by the media, as shown by the media coup against Brazilian President Dilma Rousseff in 2015, which became the breeding ground for Jair Bolsonaro's victory.
3. Daniel Kent Carrasco and Diego Bautista Páez, dossier 'An Ideological Epidemic: The Far-Right Today', *Revista Común*, 2022,

https://revistacomun.com/blog/una-epidemia-ideologica-las-ultraderechas-en-el-mundo-actual/.

4. This clarification is important insofar as the right–left divide has been called into question since the spread of cisheteropatriarchal authoritarianism beyond the right, defended by figures on the global left such as Andrés Manuel López Obrador (AMLO) in Mexico or Nayib Armando Bukele in El Salvador. These are just two heads of state with apparently left-wing agendas who are reclaiming conservatism on issues of gender and sexuality and publicly rejecting, even criminalising, feminist and LGBTQ+ movements, their demands and their rights.

5. Nicolás Alonso, *'Milo Yiannopoulos, el agitador de la extrema derecha que fue demasiado radical'* ['Milo Yiannopoulos, the Far-Right Agitator Who Was Too Radical'], *El País*, 22 February 2017, https://elpais.com/internacional/2017/02/22/estados_unidos/1487733344_889562.html.

6. This is demonstrated by the number of murders committed against the transgender community in Mexico, which ranks second in the world for murders of transgender women. In 2022, the NGO Letra Ese confirmed that from 2018 to 2022, 270 trans women were murdered in the country; *'México es el segundo país con más asesinatos de personas trans en el mundo después de Brasil'*, *Infobae*, 26 June 2022, www.infobae.com/america/mexico/2022/06/26/mexico-es-el-segundo-pais-con-mas-asesinatos-de-personas-trans-en-el-mundo-despues-de-brasil/.

7. See the video 'LEY TRANS. Intervención de Amelia Valcárcel en la COPE (26/Oct/22)', FemSocialistas, YouTube, 27 October 2022, www.youtube.com/watch?v=x9ugq7YmoYg.

8. Sophie Perry, 'Gender Critical Activist Quotes Adolf Hitler in Speech Against Trans Rights at Posie Parker Rally', *Pink News*, 16 January 2023, www.thepinknews.com/2023/01/16/newcastle-let-women-speak-rally-adolt-hitler-trans-speech/.

9. Sayak Valencia and Liliana Falcón, 'From Gore Capitalism to Snuff Politics: Necropolitics in the USA–Mexican Border' in Ariadna Estévez (ed.), *Necropower in North America: The Legal Spatialization of Disposability and Lucrative Death* (Basingstoke: Palgrave Macmillan, 2021), 35–59. My proposal is that 'regressive

sensibility' is characterised by the desire for a right-wing life, that is, the desire for a life that subscribes to fascism 2.0 not as a strong ideology, but as 'a reduction of conservative drives to what critical thinking has defined as the "authoritarian personality": a combination of fear and frustration and a lack of self-confidence that lead to the enjoyment of one's own submission'; Enzo Traverso, *'Espectros del fascismo. Pensar las derechas radicales en el siglo XXI'* ['Spectres of Fascism: Thinking about the Radical Right in the Twenty-First Century'], *Marxismo Crítico*, 6 September 2016, no. 58, https://biblat.unam.mx/hevila/HerramientaBuenosAires/2016/no58/15.pdf. Today, this regressive sensibility is crystallised in the reinforcement of gender binarism and sexual essentialism, the rise of religious fanaticism in politics, the criminalisation of abortion, the defence of the White, heterosexual nation and the explosive growth of xenophobia in the United States and around the world.

10. See the profound and erudite work on the issue by transfeminist biotechnologist Lu Ciccia, *La invención de los sexos. Cómo la ciencia puso el binarismo en nuestros cerebros y cómo los feminismos pueden ayudarnos a salir de ahí* [*The Invention of the Sexes: How Science Put Binary in Our Brains and How Feminism Can Help Us Break Out From It*] (Buenos Aires: Siglo XXI Editores, 2022).

11. Angela Davis, *Women, Race and Class* (New York: Random Books, 1981).

12. Pilar Coloma Aceña, *'Lo personal es político. El surgimiento del feminismo radical en Estados Unidos (1967–1970)'* ['The Personal is Political: The Rise of Radical Feminism in the United States (1967–1970)'], *Filanderas: Revista Interdisciplinar de Estudios Feministas* 7 (2022): 118, https://doi.org/10.26754/ojs_filanderas/fil.202278582.

13. Aingeru Mayor, Aitzole Araneta, Alicia Ramos, et al., *Transfeminismo o barbarie* [*Transfeminism or Barbarism*] (Madrid: Kaótica Libros, 2020), 8.

14. Carmen Romero Bachiller, *'¿Quién le teme al transfeminismo?'* ['Who's Afraid of Transfeminism?'], *Transfeminismo o barbarie* (Madrid: Kaótica Libros, 2020), 33.

15. Sayak Valencia, *'Del Queer al Cuir: ostranénie geopolítica y epistémica desde el sur g-local'* ['From Queer to Cuir: Geopolitical and Epis-

temic Defamiliarization from the G-local South'], in Fernando R. Lanuza and Raúl M. Carrasco (eds), *Queer & Cuir. Políticas de lo irreal* [*Queer and Cuir: Politics of the Unreal*] (Mexico: Universidad Autónoma de Querétaro/Editorial Fontamara, 2015).

16. Nuria Alabao, '*El fantasma de la Teoría Queer sobrevuela el feminismo*' ['The Ghost of Queer Theory Hovers over Feminism'], in *Transfeminismo o barbarie* (Madrid: Kaótica Libros, 2020), 145.

17. Achille Mbembe, *Necropolitics* (Durham, NC: Duke University Press, 2019).

18. The word is significant, since it encloses colonial imaginaries that reveal the colonial repetition that links the fifteenth century to the twenty-first century, with its technologies and algorithms, in terms of the production of the disposability of certain subalternised bodies, while the connection between the colonial dimension, fascism 2.0 and feminism hostile to trans rights is becoming increasingly obvious.

19. Franco Berardi, 'Prólogo', in Irmgard Emmelhainz, *La tiranía del sentido común. La reconversión neoliberal de México* [*The Tyranny of Common Sense: The Neoliberal Reconversion of Mexico*] (Mexico: Paradiso Ediciones, 2016), 12.

20. We define '*cuir*' as Sayak Valencia does, as 'a defamiliarisation of the term queer, that is, a de-automation of the reader's gaze and registers a geopolitical inflexion towards the south, a locus of enunciation with a decolonial inflexion, both playfully and critically' (2015); see Rafael Mendes Silva, 'Queer/Cuir Poetry Now: Launch of New Reading Group', Trinity College Dublin, 29 January 2025, www.tcd.ie/trinitylongroomhub/news/2025/queercuir-poetry-now-blog/.

21. Translator's note: the literal meanings for these are: trans/gay/sex worker/lesbian/mixed-race/migrant/low-waged.

22. Sayak Valencia, *Gore Capitalism*, trans. John Pluecker (Los Angeles: Semiotext(e)/MIT Press, 2018).

23. Alejandra Castillo, *Disensos feministas* [*Feminist Dissents*] (Santiago: Editorial Palinodia, 2016), 89.

24. Félix Guattari and Suely Rolnik, *Micropolítica: Cartografías del deseo* [*Micropolitics: Cartographies of Desire*] (Madrid: Traficantes de Sueños, 2006).

TRULY RADICAL

25. Audre Lorde, *Sister Outsider: Essays and Speeches* (Trumansburg, NY: Crossing Press, 1988), 91.

26. Ibid.

27. Ibid.

28. Translator's note: A reference to theorist Gloria Anzaldúa and her 1980 text, 'Speaking in Tongues, a Letter to Third World Writers', in which she evokes the situation of enunciation and writing of Third World women, marked by material and linguistic precariousness, which renders their speech and writing as inaudible as the glossolalia of mystics and alienated people who 'speak in tongues'. Included in Cherríe L. Moraga and Gloria E. Anzaldúa (eds), *This Bridge Called My Back: Writings by Radical Women of Color* (Berkeley, CA: Third Woman Press, 2002).

29. Virginia Villaplana and Berta Sichel, *Cárcel de amor: Relatos culturales en torno a la violencia de género* [*Prison of Love: Cultural Tales Around Gender Violence*] (Madrid: Museo Nacional Centro de Arte Reina Sofía, 2005), 69.

30. Valeria Flores, *Tropismos de la disidencia* [*Tropisms of Dissent*] (Santiago: Palinodia, 2017), 36.

31. Barbara Cameron, 'Gee, You Don't Seem Like an Indian', in Cherríe L. Moraga and Gloria E. Anzaldúa (eds), *This Bridge Called My Back: Writings by Radical Women of Color* (Berkeley, CA: Third Woman Press, 2002), 50.

32. Guattari and Rolnik, *Micropolítica*, 101.

33. Julieta Paredes, *Hilando fino desde el feminismo comunitario* [*Fine Spinning from Community Feminism*] (Mexico, Cooperativa El Rebozo, Zapateándole, Lente Flotante, En cortito que's pa largo and AliFem AC, 2013).

34. Ochy Curiel, *La nación heterosexual: Análisis del discurso jurídico y el régimen heterosexual desde la antropología de la dominación* [*The Heterosexual Nation: Analysis of Legal Discourse and the Heterosexual Regime Using the Anthropology of Domination*] (Bogota: Editorial Brecha Lésbica/En la Frontera, 2013).

35. Cristina Rivera Garza, *Liliana's Invincible Summer* (London: Bloomsbury, 2023), 18.

6

Intifada (انتفاضة) and the Feminist Imagination

Zahra Ali

Intifada (انتفاضة), 'uprising' in Arabic, comes from the root *nefada* (نفض), which literally means to shake something until whatever is attached to it falls off. If we cut the word in two, we obtain *inti*, the feminine pronoun for 'you' (انتِ) and *fada*, the verb 'to shake'. *Intifada* is a feminine noun in Arabic, though in French it has become masculine. To name something is also to define and situate it. The word *intifada* also frequently refers to the struggle of the Palestinian people and their resistance to Zionist occupation. The reflection I would like to make here belongs to a political tradition that places questions of decolonial emancipation at the heart of feminist thinking.

I shall therefore begin by decentring French (and English) to think about emancipation and feminisms on the basis of a term that corresponds to the political imaginary of the Arab worlds and particularly that of Iraq. However, I am not comfortable with the way it is often used in both Arab and non-Arab contexts that associate the word *intifada* with resistance movements that are led, above all, by men. By remarking on the element *inti* (انتِ), I emphasise the importance not only of recentring women but also questions of gender and sexualities.

The use of the feminine here does not invoke an essentialising differentialism of some kind, but rather a will to place at the centre minoritised and marginalised bodies, experiences and spaces that have been dominated by systems of power that are not limited to the imagined universal patriarchy. This is far from a so-called '*inter*national' feminism that lays claim to a homogenous sisterhood bringing all women together, but which in reality corresponds to an agenda and a model that is neoliberal, bourgeois and White. I prefer the term *trans*national, where 'trans' signals the idea of transcending, of shaking-off (*nefada*) and of calling into question the frontiers of nations, of gender and of sexualities. This is also to transcend the limits of the notion of 'women's rights' and their use for racist, classist and neocolonial ends, to speak above all of emancipation and liberation. To pose the problem in other terms: which rights does it concern, for which women, and on whose backs (which women)?

By *trans*national feminism, I seek to break with the idea of a 'here' and an 'over there' corresponding to an imaginary geography cultivated by the hegemonic feminisms of the North. Here (read: among civilised Whites) women have rights, not like over there (read: among barbarian non-Whites). The men from here must liberate the women from over there from the men from over there.[1] This dichotomy, which creates and reifies difference on the basis of a supposed culture or religion that sets civilised and barbarians against each other, lies at the heart of the White, neoliberal, feminist imagination. It depoliticises the differences only to ethnicise them instead, and above all camouflages what is hidden behind this geographic imaginary. In reality, there is no 'here' or 'over there', there is a Whole-World,[2] in which we all live. The difference between some women and others corresponds much more to the 'where' and to the 'how' they situate themselves in the systems of capitalist, heteropatriarchal, racial and colonial power that characterise the contemporary world. It is a matter of situating bodies, experiences and spaces at the centre and on the margin, those that are nourished by these systems and those on whose shoulders they rest alike. There are those women who obtain privileges from it, and those who are oppressed by it, those who benefit from it and those on whom the exploitation falls.

More concretely, in Iraq (as in Afghanistan),[3] it was the US imperialist interventions that culminated in the 2003 invasion that deprived women (and men) of the basic services and infrastructure they need for a dignified existence.[4] These military interventions created the conditions for the expression of the most brutal forms of heteropatriarchy and misogyny that deprived Iraqis of their freedom and their basic rights. That is to say, it was the men and women from 'here' who, under cover of democracy and feminism, literally destroyed the very possibility of a dignified life in Iraq. To place the struggles of Iraqi women at the heart of our reflection means starting from the place that the global systems of power operate, and the privileged position of these women to dismantle them.

The Global North, its middle class, its infrastructures and its economic system rely on the colonial and neocolonial exploitation of the Global South. Western democracies are based on the extraction of oil and gas that comes in its majority from the Middle East.[5] Iraq is a space at the heart of global economic and political dynamics. The country, which had the most advanced infrastructure, institutions and services such as health and education in the entire region, has been ravaged by imperialist interventions. First of all, there was the repression of the revolutionary left in the 1960s and the Western support for the Ba'athist dictatorship until the 1980s, the military and economic offensives in the 1990s, and the invasion and occupation by US-led forces in 2003. For over 50 years, the everyday lives of Iraqi men and women have been defined by war and an unprecedented economic and political brutalisation.

Nevertheless, the country has a long and rich history of insurrection, with the 1920 uprising against the British colony, followed by the great anti-imperialist demonstrations of the 1940s. Its feminist movements were anti-imperialist, and among the most radical in the region until the Ba'ath party came to power.[6] There were also uprisings against the dictatorship of Saddam Hussein, notably in 1991, which were met with mass repression. And the popular revolts in the South, notably against the political system and the elite put in place by the US administration in 2003, culminated in 2019 with *Thawra Teshreen* (the October Revolution).

Here I propose to enrich the theoretical and political feminist imagination by reflecting on and around *Thawra Teshreen*. I am not using the Iraqi context as a case study for application of a Eurocentric, White frame of reference. On the contrary, I seek to break with this well-established tendency among feminist writings from the Global North of only referring to the Global South as an example or as a field of study for which the theory is generated in the universities or intellectual milieux of the North. The Global North – or more precisely, Europe and North America – develop theoretical frameworks for which the countries of the South are merely the raw material. Instead, here I wish to give the leading role to the subjectivities, to the bodies, to the experiences and to the struggles of Iraqi protestors. It is a question of situating those women and men – whose lives are considered insignificant, easily erased, brutalised and wiped out by the colonial, heteropatriarchal and extractivist capitalist system – at the heart of the theoretical and political feminist imagination.

Rethinking feminisms through struggles in Iraq, undoing hegemonic knowledge

Postcolonial and decolonial studies, especially feminist ones,[7] have enriched our ideas about the relations between knowledge, research,[8] space/time,[9] and positionality.[10] How do we know what we know? What counts as knowledge and theory and what does not count? These are essential questions concerning the relationships between knowledge and power, political economy and the geopolitics of knowledge. It is also a matter of the material, structural and infrastructural conditions of the production and circulation of knowledge. It is clear, as the feminist Amina Mama has written with regard to the African context in her important article 'Is it Ethical to Study Africa?',[11] that what we call the global university in reality refers to publications in English and in French in journals based in the great cities of Europe and the United States. This university world produces a knowledge from the outside on the 'Middle East', on 'Iraq', above all in English, which responds to questions formulated far from these places and which develops theoretical frameworks that nevertheless come to hold sway over the region itself.

Arjun Appadurai, following Edward Said,[12] refers to concepts such as 'tribe', 'civil society' and 'honour', developed in the metropolises of the Global North and arbitrarily transferred to the realities of the Global South with no real connection to the societies concerned, revealing little more than the imagination or what he calls the 'whims' of an intellectual.[13] Yet, these concepts are repeated until they become in a sense hegemonic and are eventually taught in academic and intellectual circles in the South.

We encounter a similar tendency in feminist knowledge of the Arab worlds originating in the Global North, where 'problem-spaces'[14] and theoretical frameworks forged elsewhere are imprinted on Arab-majority societies. Yet, feminist theories are the product of political struggles that were waged first in the streets before being institutionalised in universities; they are and always have been transnational and respond to global realities, because to theorise is to create meaning, emotionally and politically, and not to produce abstract and easily relocatable ideas.

Critical feminist approaches have helped to call into question not only the universality of knowledge, but also this idea that theory is something that exists outside of people: all knowledge is situated. These critical approaches have clearly shown that behind universalism, behind this claim to rationality, far from emotions, bodies, spaces and power relations, stands a well-off White man whose knowledge is in reality not objective, but just very well situated.

Iraqi feminist knowledge has always been transnational and has laid bare the political and social struggles the country has undergone. By way of example, one of the most important feminist books in Iraq is one by Naziha al-Dulaimi, a communist militant, first woman minister in the Arab world, and a founding member of the Iraqi Women's League. In her book *Al-Mar'a al-'Iraqiyya* (*The Iraqi Woman*), published in 1952, she develops a Marxist and feminist approach connecting the struggles for social justice, class justice, anti-imperialism and feminism.[15] The next most significant book was by Sabiha Al-Shaikh Dawood, *Awwal al-Tariq illa al-Nahda al-Neswiyya fi al-Iraq* (*First Steps Towards the Feminist Renaissance in Iraq*), published just before the 1958 revolution.[16] This text represents the nationalist feminist tradition, where the notion of social class is not as central as in Naziha al-Dulaimi's book. These works reveal only a small part of the revolutionary effervescence among women during that period, of what was happening in the streets. The ideas they mobilise are neither authentically their own nor foreign, but rather the fruit of struggles and debates that create meaning, as well as of transnational and world dynamics.

Today too, feminist struggles in Iraq produce knowledge and critical theories.[17] In *Women and Gender in Iraq*, I demonstrate, for example, how feminists have appropriated the notion of gender, which originated in neoliberal UN programmes, and turned it into a feminist tool.[18] I also call into question the dichotomy between secular and religious, so central in works on feminist movements in the region, showing that this does not help us to understand the realities experienced by women and feminists in Iraq.

My principal criticism of feminist works on Iraq, particularly from a decolonial perspective, is that the emphasis on the discursive has sidelined any real reflection on the resonance and relevance of certain theoretical frameworks. While it is essential to criticise the culturalist and orientalist approach, it is equally essential to allow the categories of analysis to emerge from everyday life, from its materiality and its spatiality. A critical feminist methodology can, in a sense, consist of an analytical application of the mantra 'the personal is political' in the attentive study of everyday life, of the material spaces of life, freed from predefined analytical frameworks and notions such as nationalism and Islamism, which are often mobilised in the Iraqi context. By letting the categories emerge from the everyday reality of women and feminist activists, it is possible to go beyond the dichotomies between discursive and material, private and public, local and global, secular and religious.

However, it is clear that undoing knowledge demands first of all positioning oneself close to the social and political struggles. Feminist knowledge is formulated in action and takes shape on the street, with or without reference to the term feminism, or even by refusing to use it. Feminist knowledge in Iraq has emerged as an integral part of social, economic and political struggles that concern society as a whole. In a certain sense, Iraqi women do not have the luxury of disconnecting their particular interests from those of the society they belong to. As such, their mass participation in the October 2019 uprising was crucial as much for the future of feminist struggles in the country as for the uprising itself.

INTIFADA (انتفاضة) AND THE FEMINIST IMAGINATION

Uprising in Iraq, a reinvention of the political

From the heights of 'Mount Uhud', a tall building looking over Tahrir Square in the centre of Baghdad, young people chant 'noured watan' (نريد وطن), 'We want a country'. This building, colloquially known as 'the Turkish restaurant', had been sitting empty for over a decade. It had acquired its new name in reference to the renowned Battle of Uhud led by the Prophet Muhammad and his army. The occupation of 'Mount Uhud' by the peaceful demonstrators, by the sheer force of will in the face of the weapons of the armed militias and security services, marked the victory of the October 2019 uprising. The men and women had come under fire from the mercenaries and security forces who have been suppressing peaceful demonstrations in the country's capital since 2011. By taking over this strategic building, floor by floor, braving death at the corner of every staircase, the demonstrators were aware of what was at stake. From the top of Mount Uhud, they could see the whole of central Baghdad, and look straight across at the Green Zone created by the US army during the 2003 invasion, surrounded by concrete walls, where the central government and the political elite reside.

The young Iraqi men and women at the front of the demonstrations in October 2019 are barely 20 years old, and have never experienced the authoritarianism of the Ba'ath party, or the trauma of the decade of war with Iran, the horror of the American bombardment in the 1990s and the widespread impoverishment following the economic sanctions imposed by the UN. These young people were born in an Iraq occupied by the US Army and its allies, their childhood was marked by sectarian war and their adolescence by the invasion of ISIS. This generation has never known the years when the country was home to the best higher education and health systems in the region, as well as powerful state institutions that provided housing, electricity and job security. Their daily lives, despite the country's vast oil reserves, are marked by water and power cuts, and they suffer from the shortcomings of public services and the health and education systems. Since 2003, all the services that were once public have been privatised and the political elite, installed in power by the US administration, hold sway over all institutions and public and private companies by means of the armed violence of their militias. Unemployment is almost certain if you are not part of a family with personal connections to the political elite, or if you are not prepared to pay the equivalent of a year's salary to a member of a party or militia that profits from widespread corruption and nepotism. These young people live in a country where, despite the organisation of so-called 'democratic' elections, they risk being killed or kidnapped if they openly criticise a politician or militia affiliated to the ruling political elite.

Most of the demonstrators come from the south of the country, particularly the marshlands decimated by wars and poverty. All the largest uprisings in Iraq have begun in Basra, the province at the centre of the country's oil extraction. In this province, the hottest in the world in the month of July 2023, there is no infrastructure, electricity and water are privatised, and unemployment, extreme poverty and a lack of basic services define everyday life. The inhabitants' only contact with the oil industry is with its toxic waste and the cancers it causes, especially among children and young people.[19] Environmental activists are threatened, kidnapped and tortured, as occurred recently in the case of Jassim Al-Asadi, who fought for the preservation of the culture and ecology of the marshes. This region, once the Mesopotamian Fertile Crescent, is inhabited by a population who have preserved ways of life organised around water and natural dwellings that date back to Sumerian times. The life that flourished in this region prior to the arrival of colonial and extractivist capitalist modernity is particularly sensitive to climate change.

October 2019 was a widespread popular revolt, led by working-class and young people, who were joined by the middle class, trade unions and activists in social and feminist movements. It opposed the everyday structural violence of a life without public services and institutions, and the armed violence of a political elite and its militias. The mass participation of women, both young students and older, transformed this uprising into a veritable popular revolution. Since at least the 1990s, the wars and economic embargo had deeply impacted Iraqi women, who bear the burden of day-to-day life and survival. As mothers, workers and caregivers, women form an infrastructure in their own right in Iraq. Decades of war and economic crisis have also transformed public space into militarised and fragmented zones that are dominated by men. Women have been subject to the control of their bodies, their movements and their lives by aggravated forms of patriarchal ideology.

Tahrir Square in Baghdad, as well as Al-Haboubi Square in Nassiriyah and other protest sites throughout the country have become places where all those who are maligned, oppressed and discriminated against can exist and prosper. Women reassert their ownership of public space through marches, demonstrations and occupations, organising among themselves to become visible and audible, standing on the front line against the brutality of the security forces or taking charge of putting up banners, caring for the injured, or cooking and cleaning. During the months that Tahrir Square is occupied, the protestors shape a new everyday life that calls into question social hierarchies and societal norms, including at the level of class or gender divisions. On Tahrir Square in Baghdad, a young middle-class woman from Mansour (a residential district) becomes friends with a young worker from

Medinat Al Sadr (a working-class neighbourhood). Lovers hold hands in the face of the live bullets.

In this setting, a new social fabric weaves itself through collective organisation, Iraqi society meets, negotiates and builds a new social contract: it is a site where the uneducated poor are equals with the educated middle class, where men and women, young and old share a space and build a common movement. In these autonomous zones, self-generated by the protestors over the course of months, public services are reinvented, the squares and monuments are cleaned and renovated, and the streets embellished with countless artistic expressions.

The level and the scope of involvement by women are remarkable, but hardly surprising. One of the first demonstrations organised after the 2003 invasion was by women protesting against the attempt to call into question the basis of their rights, the Personal Status Code. Just a few months after the US invasion, the sectarian political elite brought to power by the American administration attempted to impose a code founded on sectarianism, in place of the jurisprudence combining both Shiism and Sunnism. While they were prevented from doing so by the feminist mobilisation, the sectarian parties have never stopped trying to introduce a sectarian and conservative Personal Status Code, most recently under the 'Jaafari bill'.

The post-2003 regime may be characterised as sectarian-gendered in the sense that the Muhasasa system (a political distribution based on ethnic, religious and sectarian quotas) is not only founded on ethnic, religious and sectarian criteria but also on those of gender and sexuality. The conservative and heteropatriarchal forces do not only dominate the political spheres but also the streets, thanks to their militias and armed groups. The sectarian war of 2006–2007 and the ISIS invasion in 2014 are extreme manifestations of the sectarianism and gender violence that underlies the regime installed by the

Intifada (انتفاضة) and the Feminist Imagination

Americans in 2003. The sectarian-gendered system imposes its power by means of the division of religious communities and of the sexes, evident in the strict dress codes imposed for both men and women, while limiting mixing at both religious and gender levels.

The repression and stigmatisation of the protest movement by the Iraqi authorities are clearly heteropatriarchal and are expressed through media campaigns and on social networks, seeking to undermine the revolution by branding it 'immoral'. The revolutionaries are accused of being sexually 'corrupt' and 'depraved', and all kinds of rumours circulate about the 'illicit behaviour' of the young people in the tents set up on the protest sites. The repression targets the women, and above all the young women. The political groups and their militias attempt to dissuade women from taking part by spreading fear and terror, by kidnapping demonstrators such as Saba Mahdawi and Mari Mahammed, or killing them, such as Sara Taleb and her husband Adel, Reham Yacoob in Basra, and Zahraa Ali in Baghdad. The mobilisations organised by women are also the target of attacks on social networks. The hashtag بناتك ياوطن# (Your young women, oh country) launched at the women's protest movement on 13 February is transformed into the slogan عاهراتك ياوطن# (Your whores, oh country). On the wall of the tunnel leading to Tahrir Square, and on placards held by young women during the protests, we can read 'Women of the October Revolution are revolutionaries, not whores'.

During the first months of the October uprising, over 700 peaceful protests, mostly impoverished young men, are killed by bullets or by tear gas shells fired by the security forces, while 25,000 people are injured and hundreds kidnapped and disappeared. The lethal violence and intimidations only reinforce the determination of the protestors, and paying homage to the martyrs rapidly becomes one of their leading slogans.

Among the first to die is Safaa al Sarai, who was known as the 'son of Thanwa', in reference to his mother. 'Son of Thanwa' is now in widespread use to refer to the *Thawra Teshreen* (the revolutionaries of October), and a good number of those demonstrating choose to be designated in similar fashion, by the name of their mother, rather than their father.

The uprising reinvents politics by changing the division of the sensible and the dominant order.[20] Residents of poor neighbourhoods and regions, whose culture and way of life are stigmatised and labelled as 'uncivilised' by residents of middle-class and well-off neighbourhoods, are leading the movement and demonstrating their *madanniya* (civic-mindedness).[21] The protestors redefine the frontiers of the political, by connecting economic, social and societal oppressions that impose a conservative, limited way of life. With the slogan 'We want a country', Iraqis demand social and economic justice, functioning public services and institutions better prepared to run health, education, housing, employment and in general everything necessary for a dignified life. They also demand freedom – not to be killed because of the religion or religious group they belong to or do not belong to, freedom to dress as they want and to cross social and secular barriers, freedom of expression, and the right to difference.

The protestors not only demand change, but put it into practice in their lives by proposing new rules of behaviour and building an inclusive way of living together. *Thawra Teshreen* women come from all walks of life: from the middle-aged uneducated mother in her black abaya who cooks for the protesters, to the educated middle-class woman leading debates on electoral law reform; from young women from conservative backgrounds, to those who defy the dominant dress code. They all share a common space, develop strategies and organise the weekly demonstrations. They chant together. 'No, no, no, don't say it's shameful, the revolution is the voice of women!', conscious of the subversive character of their presence and their visibility in a context where the street has become a masculine, militarised space.

Inside some of the tents, feminist programmes are the order of the day, based on the rights of women, while in most of the other tents women are sure that *Thawra Teshreen* is already bringing about change in Iraq and that the realisation of its goals will benefit women as much as men. The feminists active at the heart of the organised groups, present at the protest sites, also respect the informal and open character of the uprising, which reject any form of affiliation. The diversity of involvement by women, whether individually or as members of women's groups, the visibility of which increases during International Women's Day on 8 March 2020, demonstrates that the old term 'the Iraqi woman', most often used by politicians in their programmes – whether secular or Islamist – has been replaced in action by the more inclusive expression 'Iraqi women'.

As a result, rather than asking whether the participation of women in the 2019 Iraqi uprising is 'feminist' or pursues a 'women's rights' agenda, it is more illuminating to ask whether it has challenged the dominant order of things, particularly through the kinds of space it generated. Similarly, rather than starting from a preconceived idea of what constitutes a 'progressive' struggle, an analysis of the different levels at which mobilisation affects social space enables us to identify what is transgressive – and in what way.

Towards a feminist intifada: Reimagining time and space

Why choose the October 2019 uprising as a framework for renewing the theoretical and political feminist imagination? The global system condemns Iraqis to be victims of structural, infrastructural and political *forces of death*[22] that reduce their existences to lives deprived of dignity, brutalised and easily erased. Iraq is a space dominated by a brutal extractivism that exhausts its resources and leaves nothing to its population but toxic waste. The hypermilitarised regime the Iraqis confront is maintained by an imperialist, heteropatriarchal capitalist world system. In a certain sense, Iraqis simply experience an aggravated version of the conservatism and military and police repression that exist everywhere.

A feminist agenda grounded in a predefined category 'woman' stands opposed to the critical feminisms I have described here. Placing Iraqi subjectivities, bodies, experiences and struggles at the centre of the feminist theoretical and political imagination means reinventing a militant geography. If we are not to confine our feminist imagination within the national borders produced by heteropatriarchal and racial capitalism, it is essential that we come to understand that the global system is based on the brutalisation of a space and its people. Iraq and the Iraqi people are not a distant 'over there' of different cultures and religions. On the contrary, through no fault of their own, they are entangled in the maintenance of the privileges and daily life of the Global North. Therefore, considered from an alternative feminist perspective, the demonstrators of October 2019 are close by, and their struggles are essential to the dismantling of a cruel and violent global system.

As we have seen, most of them come from a region where there still live, particularly in the marshes, people who have preserved pre-capitalist lifestyles. At a time when we are talking about the Anthropocene and ecological disaster, starting from the lives, subjectivities, experiences, bodies and struggles of these protestors is a way of breaking with a vision of ecological justice inspired by the White middle classes of the North. It should be remembered that it is the Global South that is most affected by climate change, while

Intifada (انتفاضة) and the Feminist Imagination

the North, which accounts for only 20 per cent of the world's population, has been responsible for more than 73 per cent of CO_2 emissions since the middle of the nineteenth century.[23] We need to break free from the framework of thinking defined by capitalist modernity and consider the long view of history. Extractivist capitalist modernity is endangering life on earth, and the human and non-human populations of southern Iraq are being hit by this brutality head-on. This means that developing a theoretical and political imagination that is not limited to the 'progressive' norms of modernity is essential to preserving life on earth. The Iraqi protestors and their demands, as well as the ancestral ways of life of the regions they come from, invite us to rethink the temporality of the world beyond the time of extractivism.

In Iraq, the uprising, although bloodily suppressed, had a considerable impact on people's daily lives and changed the societal culture and values on the streets of the country. As far as the feminist movement is concerned, it has pushed activists from established feminist networks and organisations out of their NGO comfort zone, redefining the boundaries of politics. For the demonstrators in Tahrir Square, politics is not simply the fight for legal or economic rights. It is about reclaiming space and determining for oneself the life we want to live. It is about connecting the social, the economic and the societal, as well as justice and freedom. It is about taking our place and making ourselves visible, changing the way things are shared and the dominant order. It means demonstrating what it means to live a dignified life in action, on the streets, independently and autonomously.

*Trans*national and post/decolonial critical feminist approaches tell us one thing, that there is a Whole-World, a colonial/neocolonial, racial and heteropatriarchal capitalist system that defines the boundaries of the world we live in and chooses who gets to cross them. It seems to me that despite their specificity, the fact that the protests and uprisings of October 2019 took place not only in Iraq, but also in Lebanon, Chile, Haiti and elsewhere, reminds us of the need to create connections and intersections between transnational struggles.

These movements, their strength and creativity, offer us a new political and theoretical imagination. It is in the streets first and foremost that theory is developed, because it is in the streets that theory must make sense. In Iraq, as elsewhere, many people have become aware of the gap between academics and their theories, and those who are intellectual-activists; and of the need to break with these hierarchies. These uprisings remind us of the importance of theorising not about, but with, and from, the movements themselves.[24]

I therefore call for a feminist *inti*fada that reimagines the time and space of our struggles, while no longer taking capitalist modernity as a frame of reference and developing for it a militant geography that rejects national borders and reinvents the near and the far. This *inti*fada places the uncivilised, the barbarians, at the heart of its theoretical and political imagination and emancipates itself from nationalisms and their military and security regimes. This is the struggle against the *forces of death*, whether they be political, infrastructural or social, and for freedom, in particular of the lives, bodies and experiences brutalised by the system of this Whole-World. It is a fight for the future, and for life.

Translated from French by Fionn Petch

Notes

1. A reference to the celebrated formula of Gayatri Chakravorty Spivak in 'Can the Subaltern Speak?', in Cary Nelson and Lawrence Grossberg (eds), *Marxism and the Interpretation of Culture* (Basingstoke: Macmillan Education, 1988), 271–313.

INTIFADA (انتفاضة) AND THE FEMINIST IMAGINATION

2. Édouard Glissant, *Treatise on the Whole-World*, trans. Celia Britton (Liverpool: Liverpool University Press, 2020).

3. Lila Abu-Lughod, 'Do Muslim Women Really Need Saving? Anthropological Reflections on Cultural Relativism and Its Others', *American Anthropologist* 104(3) (2002): 783–790, https://doi.org/10.1525/aa.2002.104.3.783.

4. Zahra Ali, *Women and Gender in Iraq: Between Nation-Building and Fragmentation* (Cambridge: Cambridge University Press, 2018).

5. See, for example, Joel Beinin, Bassam Haddad and Sherene Seikaly, *A Critical Political Economy of the Middle East and North Africa* (Stanford, CA: Stanford University Press, 2020); and Timothy Mitchell, *Carbon Democracy: Political Power in the Age of Oil* (London: Verso, 2023).

6. Ali, *Women and Gender in Iraq*.

7. Many such works could be cited, among them Linda Tuhiwai Smith, *Decolonizing Methodologies: Research and Indigenous Peoples* (London: Zed Books, 1999); Jacqui Alexander and Chandra Talpade Mohanty, *Feminist Genealogies, Colonial Legacies, Democratic Futures* (London: Routledge, 1997); Chandra Talpade Mohanty, *Feminism without Borders: Decolonizing Theory, Practicing Solidarity* (Durham, NC: Duke University Press, 2003); and Inderpal Grewal and Caren Kaplan (eds), *Scattered Hegemonies: Postmodernity and Transnational Feminist Practices* (Minneapolis, MN: University of Minnesota Press, 2006).

8. Ella Shohat, 'Gendered Cartographies of Knowledge: Area Studies, Ethnic Studies, and Postcolonial Studies', in Ella Shohat, *Taboo Memories, Diasporic Voices* (Durham, NC: Duke University Press, 2006), 1–16.

9. Lila Abu-Lughod, 'Zones of Theory in the Anthropology of the Arab World', *Annual Review of Anthropology* 18 (1989), 267–306, https://doi.org/10.1146/annurev.an.18.100189.001411; and Arjun Appadurai, 'Theory in Anthropology: Center and Periphery', *Comparative Studies in Society and History* 28(2) (1986): 356–61.

10. Timothy Mitchell, 'The Middle East in the Past and Future of Social Science', in David L. Szanton (ed.), *The Politics of Knowl-*

edge Production: Area Studies and the Disciplines (Berkeley, CA: University of California Press, 2002), 74–118.

11. Amina Mama, 'Is it Ethical to Study Africa? Preliminary Thoughts on Scholarship and Freedom', *African Studies Review* 50(1) (2007): 1–26, https://doi.org/10.1353/arw.2005.0122.

12. Edward Said, *Culture and Imperialism* (New York: Vintage, 1994); and Edward Said, *Orientalism* (New York: Vintage, 1979).

13. Appadurai, 'Theory in Anthropology'.

14. David Scott, *Refashioning Futures: Criticism after Postcoloniality* (Princeton, NJ: Princeton University Press, 1999).

15. Naziha Al-Dulaimi, *Al-Mar'a al-'Iraqiyya* [*The Iraqi Woman*] (Baghdad: Matba'at al-Rabitah, 1952).

16. Sabiha al-Shaikh Dawood, *Awwal al-Tariq Ila al-Nahda al-Niswiyya fi al-'Iraq* [*First Steps Towards the Feminist Renaissance in Iraq*] (Baghdad: Matba'at al-Rabitah, 1958).

17. Ali, *Women and Gender in Iraq*.

18. Ibid.

19. Mac Skelton, 'The Long Shadow of Iraq's Cancer Epidemic and COVID-19', *MERIP* 297 (Winter 2020), https://merip.org/2020/12/the-long-shadow-of-iraqs-cancer-epidemic-and-covid-19-297/; and Omar Dewachi, 'Toxicity of Life and Everyday Survival in Iraq', *Jadaliyya*, 13 August 2013, www.jadaliyya.com/Details/29295.

20. Jacques Rancière, *Le maître ignorant: Cinq leçons sur l'émancipation intellectuelle* [*The Ignorant Schoolmaster: Five Lessons in Intellectual Emancipation*], (Paris: Fayard, 1987); and Jacques Rancière, *Aux bords du politique* [*On the Shores of Politics*] (Paris: La fabrique, 1998).

21. Zahra Ali, 'Theorising Uprisings: Iraq's Thawra Teshreen', *Third World Quarterly* 45(10) (2024): 1573–88, https://doi.org/10.1080/01436597.2022.2161359.

22. I prefer the term 'forces of death' to Achille Mbembe's notion of 'necropolitics' because it allows me to refer to the infrastructures and structures essential to the preservation of life. See Zahra, 'Theorising Uprisings'.

INTIFADA (انتفاضة) AND THE FEMINIST IMAGINATION

23. For a postcolonial critique of the question of the Anthropocene, see Dipesh Chakrabarty, *The Climate of History in a Planetary Age* (Chicago, IL: University of Chicago Press, 2021).

24. I'm very involved as a researcher and as a feminist alongside intellectuals and activists in Iraq, with whom I have formed a network with the aim of 'making' critical and emancipated knowledge. We seek to think and theorise from Iraq as a social and political space, and to develop epistemological reflection based on the daily realities of Iraqis.

7

'Of Course the Word is a Weapon'

The Magazine *AWA* and the Journal *Fippu* as Platforms of Expression for Feminists in Struggle in Africa (from 1957 to the End of the 1980s)

Rama Salla Dieng

> Nostalgic songs dedicated to the African mother mixed up with men's anguish for Mother Africa are no longer enough for us.[1]

These are the words of Mariama Bâ, who posterity remembers more for her literary output – notably her 1979 novel *So Long a Letter* – than for her political action. Yet, Mariama Bâ was highly active at the heart of women's movements and associations in the young independent states of West Africa. Educated – like so many other young women from the region that was to become Mali, Senegal, Côte d'Ivoire, Cameroon, Benin, Guinea and Niger – at the École Normale de Rufisque teacher-training college (ENJF), she was one of the often-forgotten female architects of both transnational and local struggles for women's rights.[2] Alongside their more celebrated male peers, they were full participants in the political decolonisation movements. In 1946, African women from the Four Communes, who were also French citizens, became eligible to vote. Yet, paradoxically, 1946 led to the entrenchment of gender divisions in the field of political action, and deepened the political marginalisation of women in what Aminata Diaw has described as a 'republic without female citizens'.[3] In her view, the fact that men controlled both the economic resources and political forums, and that most women were still financially dependent on their male relatives increased the association of political leadership with a masculine vision. This, in turn, reinforced social expectations that women should play the role of facilitators in the public sphere, and be responsible for mediating social relations and the domestic economy, while their male counterparts took centre stage. In a context of repression by colonial authorities, and later by single-party states, political leaders organised to forge transnational solidarities, even when their two strategic priorities remained 'national unity' and 'development'. As a result of these political priorities, women political organisers and activists often conformed to the expectations of the dominant parties, in some cases even rejecting feminist discourse and accepting the patriarchal order of political institutions.[4]

The erasure of women's crucial role was also evident outside the political sphere, for example, in literary texts written in the 1950s–1970s. In this literature, which fosters male hegemony, 'women are either represented as idealised mothers or as secondary characters defined by their position in relation to men'.[5] Consequently, existing in the public sphere as a female citizen and expressing oneself there politically or artistically became strongly political gestures. These modes of expression served women to reassert their power as political actors and to formulate their demands for liberation. This is the fuller meaning of Mariama Bâ's literary formula quoted above.

In this text, I wish to revisit the political expression and participation of women in the 1947–1980 period through the magazine *AWA* and the journal *Fippu*, which were published in Senegal and distributed throughout West Africa. Following Irène d'Almeida,[6] I argue that women's activities on editorial committees were political not only in terms of their 'turning to writing' and speaking out, but also simply in terms of their presence and how they gradually took over spaces that were not designed for them.

When the word is a weapon

In Africa, women's movements played a decisive role in national liberation. One such case is Senegal, where their activism also shaped the politics of the postcolonial state (1950–1980). Yet, in Senegal, there is a historic rift between, on the one hand, traditional women's associations that pragmatically defend access to basic social services such as education, health and – to a lesser extent – political expression, without seeking to upset the established order, and, on the other hand, feminist movements that aim to reform society along more egalitarian lines. Their strategies, repertoires of action and modes of organisation are more radical. Frequently, they take an intersectional approach founded in their belief in the convergence of different struggles.

Most of the women's movements that emerged around the time of independence did not shake up the status quo of sex, gender, caste and class.[7] Their rallying cry, 'Independence above all!'[8] indicates the consensus with men that this was the priority, and that it could not take second place to other considerations, even if they were as important as fighting patriarchy. Independence was won in 1957. Yet, it left a bitter taste of continuity, a pseudo-rupture that novelist Ken Bugul (a pseudonym) perceptively expressed in her 1984 novel *The Abandoned Baobab*:

Independence disappointed me. I believed that independence was going to save me. There was no sense of identity, no breath of fresh air. Independence was like the recognition and officialisation of dependence.[9]

Over the following decade, both individually and collectively, women made their first timid steps towards publishing their writing and contributing to intellectual life in the country.[10] This period saw the emergence of *Femmes de soleil* [*Women of the Sun*] in 1957, later becoming *AWA, la Revue de la femme noire* [*AWA, the Black Woman's Review*] in January 1964.[11] A pioneering women's magazine, the editor-in-chief was the Senegalese journalist Annette Mbaye d'Erneville, supported by a team of militants for women's rights and political activists from all of West Africa, such as the Guinean Jeanne Martin Cissé, as well as writers like Virginie Kamara, who was also involved in the journal *Présence africaine* [*African Presence*].

AWA comprises one of the rare archives that documents the decision of a group of women to make use of the written press to express themselves and to reach larger audiences. The editorial choices of the magazine, as well as its deliberate silences during its overall period of activity from 1957–1976, illuminate a rich chapter in women's history, a key period for the revolutionary left and its subsequent influence on women's growing political awareness. Similarly, the views and positions expressed by another journal, *Fippu*, which emerged just as *AWA* came to the end of its run, tell us about the ideology and strategy of Yewwu-Yewwi, the feminist organisation founded in 1984 that ran it.

My argument is that African women and the feminist collectives that were active at the time negotiated liberating futures by alternating strategic 'silences' with the choice to 'speak out or write', even though they signed their articles anonymously or collectively in order to 'fight back' in the pages of *AWA* and *Fippu*. Speech and silence are far from antithetical, and 'keeping silent' is not the same as being silent.

FEMINISM FOR THE WORLD

From AWA to Fippu: Different repertoires, modes of action and expression

The editors of *AWA* seemed to aim at educating the people without challenging the status quo. They adopted a policy of transnational solidarity and sisterhood with all African and Black women, as illustrated by the review's headings 'Echoes' and 'Across the Continent'. The bulk of the magazine's readership was located in French-speaking Africa and the Black worlds, meaning it focused on feminine aesthetics and the experiences of Black women. Its covers were by and large devoted to Black women who symbolised a particular vision of femininity and Afro-modernity, such as the actor Isseu Niang, while also bringing attention to female combatants such as those of the African Party for the Independence of Guinea and Cape Verde, including Ernestina-Titina Silá, murdered on 20 January 1973 as she was travelling to the funeral of her comrade-in-arms Amílcar Cabral.

Meanwhile, the editors of the journal of the Yewwu-Yewwi movement for Women's Liberation (PLF), *Fippu*, adopted an openly feminist approach, under the guidance of the movement's president Marie-Angélique Savané and the editor-in-chief Fatoumata Sow, to help build a feminist culture of women on their feet, fighting against the patriarchal social order. *Fippu* clearly set out to give women a voice and a place in a single-sex space, unlike *AWA*, which published contributions by men. The section 'Our Bodies Ourselves' dealt with women's health and well-being, 'Women on the Move' with women's struggles in Africa, 'The Bees' with women's work, 'Our Rights' is self-evident, while 'The Creative Ones' and 'The Muses' were spaces for women to express their artistic talents; 'What They've Been Reading' shared reading recommendations,[12] while 'Tips' offered cooking recipes and other tricks. Regular contributors such as feminist journalist Eugénie Rokhaya Aw N'diaye, who died in 2022, economist Fatimatou Zahra Diop, academic Fatoumata Sow, sociologist Hélène Rama Niang and Deffa Marième Wane kept the magazine alive with provocations and protests. The articles ranged from the fight against skin whitening to an analysis of the condition of rural women, maternity leave and international solidarity. There were poems dedicated to their sister Winnie Mandela in support of the anti-apartheid struggle,[13] tributes to Thomas Sankara and later to his widow and comrade-in-struggle Mariam and their children on the news of Sankara's death.[14]

AWA: Organise and express without challenging the status quo?

AWA played a decisive role in the formation of a platform that allowed women in Francophone Africa and beyond to organise. The strategies of the editors demanded the use of pseudonyms or signing articles with a first name only, or collective publication. Sometimes they weren't signed at all when putting forward certain ideas.

AWA was anti-racist, internationalist and pan-African. It set itself the task of serving the women of Africa and the diaspora and of uniting them beyond linguistic and political boundaries. It aimed to amplify the political action of women's organisations and associations, as on the occasion that it boldly reproduced the testimony of Jeanne Martin Cissé, one of the first five General Secretaries of the African Women's Conference (CAF). The conference was arranged by the Pan-African Women's Organization (PAWO),[15] founded on 31 July 1962 in Dar es Salaam, Tanganyika, and attended by delegations from 21 African states. Jeanne Martin Cissé's statement clearly set out her ambitions and called for unity: 'We believe that regardless of ideological issues, race or creed, the women

FEMINISM FOR THE WORLD

of the world must unite. We believe that what unites them is more important than what divides them.'[16]

The decision to establish 31 July as International African Woman's Day following the first PAWO conference in Bamako, Mali, from 18–23 July 1963, was driven by this desire to acknowledge women's struggles as political struggles. The purpose of this celebration of the first pan-African women's movement was to promote the emancipation of African women in a continent where 'men and women enjoy the same political, economic and social rights'.[17]

If, unlike her former comrades in the struggle of the Union of Senegalese Women, Jeanne Martin Cissé – the first African woman to preside over the Security Council of the United Nations – was recognised and celebrated in the pages of *AWA* and elsewhere in her lifetime, the journal highlighted the contributions of other African women to major conferences at the local, national and transnational levels, as well as their professional and political achievements. *AWA* celebrated the election of four female Senegalese deputies: Caroline Faye Diop, then President of the Women's Council of the UPS (the future Socialist Party), Awa Dia Thiam, who was a political activist in the youth wing of the same party, Léna Diagne Gueye, who was a state nurse and in charge of press and information issues in the women's wing of the UPS, and Marianne Sambou Sohai, a member of the editorial staff of *AWA*.[18]

Sohai and Diop, both of whom were graduates of the ENJF in Rufisque, have left a rich legacy. Diop was involved in drafting the first Family Code in 1972, fought for the right of mothers to receive family allowances in the event of divorce, and argued for the establishment of Senegalese Women's Day on 25 March. She never ceased to reaffirm women's ambition to be political actors, even as she acknowledged that they are instrumentalised for electoral purposes:

140

We no longer want to be mere electoral voices, the ones that tilt the balance... We want to be involved in the development of our nation, take a full share of the responsibility and play our role in accepting those responsibilities.[19]

In its defence of the rights of women (and of men) and in assigning value to femininity, without taking a political nor feminist position, *AWA* embodied an ideological tension between those who fought for women's rights without the label 'feminist' and militants who openly claimed it. The paradoxical position of *AWA* on feminism was made clear in the editorial of the first issue, published in January 1964 and titled 'Reflection'. It was not signed but today we know it was written by editor-in-chief Annette Mbaya d'Erneville. In this text, she rejected the cause of equality between the sexes 'between men and women, or the emancipation of women, because women have already demonstrated their abilities'. She declared that 'it is not a matter of using *AWA* to launch a crusade for equality between women and men, nor to extol the emancipation of African women. That lies in the past, as everywhere women have proved themselves.'[20] This rejection of the feminist label by *AWA* and its members was part of a determination to avoid discord in the face of nationalist priorities. It also reflects a distancing from hegemonic white feminism and its priorities, which lay elsewhere. In this context, the focus was on the complementarity between the sexes, as the sociologist Fatou Sow recalls: 'Myself, in my first article on women published in 1963, in the first issue of *AWA*, I defended the complementarity of these relations. The inequalities denounced by women were above all those generated by the colonial and later neocolonial order.'[21]

In the following number, dedicated to the Women's Fortnight celebrations, Caroline Diop nevertheless declared herself a feminist: 'I am a feminist. I am for equality between men and women, but I'm not talking about a mathematical equality. Rather, one that is a function of the complementarity of genders.'[22] This attitude of negotiation (a kind of Obioma Nnaemeka-style nego-feminism) bears the stamp of the education they had received in Rufisque from their teacher Germaine Le Goff, who had prepared them to serve the nation and to teach as model citizens.

While they have often appeared conciliatory, at the risk of appearing less 'political', it seems to me that the women editors of *AWA*, through their writing, publishing, popular education, dance, involvement in community life, cinema, cooking, teaching and building the young nation, adopted a number of strategies to advance their causes without betraying the overriding objectives of achieving national unity and 'development'. In so doing, they became political protagonists advancing the causes of women at the local, national and transnational levels.

Fippu: Standing up against the patriarchal social order

In January 1984, 16 left-wing revolutionary women militants established Yewwu-Yewwi for the liberation of women, the first radical feminist 'influence movement', with the idea of 'bringing about a new awareness of the need to fight to change mentalities'. One of its founders, Marie-Angélique Savané, joined the Soroptimist club's meetings in 1975, at the invitation of Annette Mbaye of *AWA*. According to her, Yewwu-Yewwi's aim was to devise a feminist social project in reaction to the dominant discourse of women within Soroptimist clubs, Zonta, and other women's associations, which failed to criticise the subordination of women within capitalism (or even socialism as it was theorised and practised in Senegal at the time). During our interview in 2019, she recalled what differentiated them from other women's movements:

> The creation of Yewwu-Yewwi came in response to the previous women's associations because we couldn't make them understand concepts such as the patriarchy or the subordination of women to capitalism, even within left-wing parties. I remain convinced that we have to look at the most fundamental aspects of society, its very roots, in order to transform it.[23]

Created by left-wing militants, Yewwu-Yewwi sought to incorporate the masses and to overcome divisions of class, sex, generation, caste or between city and countryside. It pursued a whole range of strategies, from awareness-raising to lobbying by way of civil disobedience. Yewwu-Yewwi was not dependent on international funding and was therefore able to define and implement its own autonomous programme, unlike other women's organisations.[24] Its radical and intersectional feminist positions were transgressive. The group held public debates on the reform of the Family Code, polygamy and the right to abortion, an audacious subject to address at the time. From 1984 to 1987, it defended the recognition of International Women's Day on 8 March in Senegal, held conferences on contraception, feminism in Senegal, women and mental health, women and Islam, and much more.

'OF COURSE THE WORD IS A WEAPON'

The movement established a prize for political work towards the emancipation of women, and denounced sexist violence. Its magazine *Fippu* – a word which means rebellion and rupture – served as a tribune and platform for forging transnational alliances with other feminist groups.

Fippu's mission was to act as a sounding box for the words of women in struggle and to raise awareness, as recalled in the collective text 'Appeal to the women of Senegal' written in December 1983. The text denounced the multidimensional oppression and exploitation of women in Africa: marital oppression, the oppression of motherhood, cultural oppression, exploitation in factories as menial labour, in the services sector, in cities as domestic servants or prostitutes, etc.[25] The authors recalled that these evils had been denounced prior to independence by an educated fringe, but that the longed-for independence had offered privileges to this minority of educated women, while leaving behind the 'disadvantaged' women who were insufficiently aware of the subordination they lived under due to the patriarchy and male hegemony. Although some social action has been taken, women have remained on the margins of political and economic decision-making bodies. Hence, Yewwu-Yewwi's 15-point programme for the liberation of women, based on an 'acute awareness' of the oppression and exploitation they suffer in society, and on the fact that they alone are in a position to undertake and win this struggle.

In a text titled 'Dare, and We Can Take It',[26] they laid claim to 'the other word' to bring about the liberation of all:

With thirst, because we've been deprived of it for too long.
With delicacy and voluptuousness, because it is fragile, volatile and loving.
With firmness, because it grants the power of transformation.

What is it? The other word.

The one that women excluded from the public sphere have for centuries murmured, whispered, sung and shouted.

In homes, in the fields, in harems, in kitchens, by wells and streams, in the sacred woods.

The other word, not to enslave or to take revenge.

But to discover, push back the frontiers of ignorance, of stupidity and prejudice.

The other word, to seek, within a reimagined equality, a different way of being a woman, of being a man, of living in partnership.

Fippu is the reflection and spark of such a quest.

The expression of a dynamic of liberation between the sexes and in society that leaves no question unanswered, that dodges no debate.

Fippu will be the journal of feminist alternative communication.

Fippu will be one of the paths that lead to the wonderful yet possible dream, of a new dawn.

So come, come with us!

A vibrant invitation to forge links, to join a community of women standing on their feet in struggle, but also, and above all, an invitation to action. The invocation of this 'other word' echoes that of the Cameroonian feminists of the Collectif des femmes pour le renouveau (CFR) with whom Yewwu-Yewwi had worked, notably at the Nairobi conference in 1985, where together they affirmed their rejection of an agenda giving priority to 'development'. The 'other word' also expresses their refusal to be seen as the female protectors of patriarchal social norms.

Internationalism allied with local action was the modus operandi of Yewwu-Yewwi, as we can see in the pages of *Fippu*, through texts such as '10 Years of International

Feminism, An Overview from Mexico (1975) to Nairobi (1985)'[27] by Savané, or 'When the Pen Becomes a Weapon' by Eugénie Rokhaya Aw and Fatoumata Sow, which discussed two feminist magazines from the Maghreb (Morocco's *8 Mars* and Tunisia's *Nissa*).[28] In addition to declaring their solidarity with the anti-apartheid struggle in South Africa, they took part in the festivities for the fourth anniversary of the Burkina Faso revolution in August 1987, with a delegation of ten women from Yewwu-Yewwi among the guests of honour of President Thomas Sankara, tragically assassinated on 15 October that same year. Deffa Marième Wane, in her account of this visit to Burkina Faso titled 'In the Country of Integrated Women',[29] emphasises that Sankara issued the following call to exhort them to break their chains:

Down with polygamy!
Down with female circumcision!
Down with forced marriage!
Feudal husbands? Re-educate them!
Rotten husbands? Bin them!
Forward with the Burkinabe women's revolution!
For the solidarity and liberation of African women?
  Onwards and upwards!
Thank you, Comrade!

Recognising that feminism is not yet a 'product of current consumption' in their country, the members of Yewwu-Yewwi took their time to define themselves as a feminist collective in a text titled 'Who We Are',[30] which appeared in *Fippu*: 'Women of diverse religions and ethnicities, married, divorced and single. Some are mothers, some childless: a snapshot of the different statuses of women who exist in Senegal. Professional women, as well as unemployed women and students.' The authors reaffirm their independence from political parties, given they were often presented as the women's arm of the revolutionary left-wing party And-Jëf/PADS (African Party for Democracy and Socialism) – which explains the silence of *Fippu* on party-political questions, even if their content was self-evidently political and cross-cutting.

Instead, it focused on bringing to light the challenges facing Senegalese women in the workplace, in the legal system, as citizens, in the banking system, in religion, whether in cities or in rural areas. For example, a reportage on the women of Boucotte Wolof, a village close to Ziguinchor, who were working together to establish a market gardening collective to reduce their dependence on the rice and millet crops that climate conditions and drought were making impossible. Or the dossier on the Senegalese Family Code published in October 1987, followed by a text from Fatoumata Sow, 'One more to improve', on the reform to this code to strengthen and expand the rights of women.[31]

Yewwu-Yewwi helped prepare the next generation of feminist activists, through its intersectional critique of the exploitation and oppression of women and men in a patriarchal context dominated by a single political party and the hegemonic advance of capitalism.

Not by way of a conclusion: The political legacies of AWA and Fippu

In Senegal and French-speaking West Africa, social movements, associations, women's unions and political activists have played a part in raising awareness and building a political community of women that transcends divisions of race, caste, class and sexuality, by placing collective empowerment at the heart of the project to liberate and build nations in the wake of independence. Their members are invested in the construction of networks of alliance and transnational political action, col-

'OF COURSE THE WORD IS A WEAPON'

lective support structures as well as spaces of expression that survived them. This legacy has sharpened feminist political awareness and made their emancipation possible, in particular by going beyond the domestic economy that was central to the training of young indigenous women just after independence, to incorporate solidarity and sisterhood.[32] These political activists understood the need for an intersectional approach to pan-Africanism, which echoes the position of the historian Ama Biney: 'An anti-patriarchal consciousness, alongside an anti-capitalist and anti-imperialist stance, must be the agenda of the pan-Africanists of the 21st century'.[33]

Although it asserted its female focus, *AWA* did not take a political or feminist stance. The magazine did, however, inspire an openly feminist generation of political leaders and activists through its explicit and implicit positions. *Fippu*, for its part, positioned itself on the far-left and saw its political action as a 'speaking out' or 'fighting back'. Both were political in terms of their content, but also because the women they brought together 'acted' in public spaces to which they had had to force access in some way. It is no coincidence that Annette d'Erneville's first collection of poems, published in 1965 under the title *Poèmes africains*, was republished in 1966 under the title *Kaddu* ('word' in Wolof).

Two years later, the first female director of a feature film in Africa, the ethnographer Safi Faye, released her film *Kaddu Beykat (Voice of the Peasant)*, focused on voices from the rural world, specifically those of the peasant farmers of her rural Serer village Fad'Jal. Here too, the emphasis was on speaking out and challenging the political leaders of the day, whose economic policies were having a major impact on the livelihoods of the peasantry.[34] In 1978, Awa Thiam, a Senegalese anthropologist and co-founder of the Coordination des femmes noires, published *La Parole aux Négresses*[35] in which she challenged the leaders of negritude, who were

149

known for celebrating the beauty of Black women, as in Senghor's famous poem 'Femme nue, femme noire',[36] but who remained deaf to their political demands. She formulated a theory of intersectionality before the term was fashionable, analysing the problems faced by African and Black women in their private lives, polygamy, genital mutilation, gender-based violence and skin whitening, at the risk of betraying 'the secrets of the tribe'.[37]

> Speak up to face up. Speak up to express your refusal, your revolt. Render words active. Word-action. Subversive word. ACT-ACT-ACT, joining theoretical practice to practical practice.[38]

In 1979, Mariama Bâ, another graduate of the Rufisque school, encouraged by her 'sister' Annette Mbaye d'Erneville, published her first novel, which went on to become a classic of African and feminist literature. This was treating writing as a means of liberation that Mariama Bâ justified with this lucid formula: 'Of course books are weapons!'[39] Later, it was Annette Mbaye who encouraged in turn another Senegalese writer, Mariétou Mbaye Biléoma, to publish her *The Abandoned Baobab* in 1984. This expressed all of her creative genius, and secured her place in the history of rebellious women, under the pen name of Ken Bugul.

Acknowledgements

To the members of Yewwu-Yewwi who kindly agreed to talk to me and to Tabara Korka Ndiaye for making the digitised covers of *Fippu* available to me; to Ruth Bush and Claire Ducournau for digitising the issues of *AWA*, www.awamagazine.org/fr/index-des-magazines/.

Translated from French by Fionn Petch

Notes

1. Mariama Bâ, '*Fonction des littératures africaines écrites*' ['The Function of Written African Literature'], *Écriture française dans le monde* 3(5) (1981): 7.

2. Diane L. Barthel, 'The Rise of a Female Professional Elite: The Case of Senegal', *African Studies Review* 18(3) (1975): 1–17; Pascale Barthélémy, '*Instruction ou éducation?: La formation des Africaines à l'École normale d'institutrices de l'AOF de 1938 à 1958*' ['Instruction or Education? The Training of African Women at the French West African Teacher Training College from 1938 to 1958'], *Cahiers d'études africaines* (2003): 371–388, https://doi.org/10.4000/etudesafricaines.205; and Annette Mbaye d'Erneville, *Femmes Africaines: Propos recueillis par Annette Mbaye d'Erneville, suivi de une si longue lettre par Mariama Bâ* [*African Women: Comments Collected by Annette Mbaye d'Erneville, Followed by a Considerably Long Letter by Mariama Bâ*] (Romorantin: Éditions Martinsart, 1981).

3. Momar-Coumba Diop (ed.), *Gouverner le Sénégal: Entre ajustement structurel et développement durable* [*Governing Senegal: Between Structural Adjustment and Sustainable Development*] (Paris: Karthala, 2004), 230–236.

4. Fatou Sow, '*Mouvements féministes en Afrique*' ['Feminist Movements in Africa'], *Revue Tiers Monde* 209(1) (2012): 145–160, https://doi.org/10.3917/rtm.209.0145.

5. Carole Boyce-Davies and Molara Ogundipe-Leslie (eds), *Moving Beyond Boundaries: Black Women's Diasporas* (New York: NYU Press, 1995), vol. 2, 137.

6. Irène Assiba d'Almeida, *Francophone African Women Writers: Destroying the Emptiness of Silence* (Gainesville, FL: University Press of Florida, 1994).

7. Rama Salla Dieng, 'From Yewwu Yewwi to #FreeSenegal: Class, Gender and Generational Dynamics of Radical, Feminist Activism in Senegal', *Politics & Gender* 20(2) (2024): 478–484, https://doi.org/10.1017/S1743923X2200071X.

8. Fatou Sarr, '*Féminismes en Afrique occidentale ? Prise de conscience et luttes politiques et sociales*' ['Feminisms in West Africa? Aware-

FEMINISM FOR THE WORLD

ness and Political and Social Struggles'], in Christine Verschuur and Deepika Bahri (eds), *Vents d'Est, vents d'Ouest: Mouvements de femmes et féminismes anticoloniaux* [*East Winds, West Winds: Women's Movements and Anticolonial Feminisms*] (Geneva: Graduate Institute Publications, 2016), 79–100.

9. Ken Bugul, *Le Baobab fou* [*The Abandoned Baobab*] (Dakar: Nouvelles éditions africaines, 1984).

10. Ndèye Sokhna Guèye, *Mouvements sociaux des femmes au Sénégal*, CODESRIA, Conseil pour le développement de la recherche en sciences sociales en Afrique, 2015.

11. For more on *AWA*, see the blog *African Reading Cultures* by Ruth Bush and Claire Ducournau, www.africanreadingcultures.org/fr/publications-2/.

12. Sometimes critical, such as the review of Aminata Sow Fall's *L'expère de la Nation* [*The Former Father of the Nation*], by Hélène Rama Niang in *Fippu* 1 (August 1987): 29.

13. *Fippu* 1 (August 1987): 19.

14. *Fippu* 2 (April 1989): 17–20.

15. PAWO's founders include many former ENFJ students from Rufisque: Jeanne Martin Cissé, Nima Sow and Fatou Toure from Guinea, Jeanne Gervais from Côte d'Ivoire, Aoua Keita from Mali, and Virginie Camara and Caroline Diop from Senegal. PAWO contributed to the creation of the Organization of African Unity (OAU) the following year. Also present were delegations from the South African Pan-African Congress and the African National Congress, Tanganyika and Zanzibar, the Algerian National Liberation Front, the Mozambican Liberation Front (FRELIMO), the Popular Movement for the Liberation of Angola (MPLA), the African Party for the Independence of Guinea and Cape Verde (PAIGC), the two main Zimbabwean parties ZAPU and ZANU, etc.

16. *AWA* 1 (January 1964): 12.

17. *AWA* 2 (March 1964): 13.

18. *AWA* 3 (new series) (February 1973): 27.

19. *AWA* 1 (January 1964): 16.

20. Editorial, *AWA* 1 (January 1964): 3.

'OF COURSE THE WORD IS A WEAPON'

21. Fatou Sow, *Revue Tiers Monde, Mouvements féministes en Afrique* 209(1) (2012): 145–160.
22. *AWA* 2 (March 1964): 16.
23. Interview with the author, May 2019.
24. Oumar Kane and Hawa Kane, 'The Origins of the Feminist Movement in Senegal: A Social History of the Pioneering Yewwu-Yewwi', *African Sociological Review* 22(1) (2018): 18–30.
25. 'Visions' section, *Fippu* 1 (August 1987): 7.
26. 'Des mots pour nous dire' section, *Fippu* 1 (August 1987): 5.
27. 'Femmes en mouvement' section, *Fippu* 1 (August 1987): 26.
28. *Fippu* 1 (August 1987): 28.
29. 'Et si Yewwu Yewwi nous était conté' section, *Fippu* 2 (April 1989): 7.
30. 'Visions' section, *Fippu* 2 (April 1989): 5–7.
31. 'Nos voix' section, *Fippu* 2 (April 1989): 8–9.
32. Rama Salla Dieng, *Féminismes africains: Une histoire décoloniale* (Paris: Présence africaine, 2021).
33. Ama Biney, 'Pan-Africanism, Intersectionality and African Problems', *Journal of Southern African Studies* 48(2) (2022): 400, https://doi.org/10.1080/03057070.2022.2065770.
34. Rama Salla Dieng, 'The Land Doesn't Lie', *Africa Is a Country*, trans. Ndeye Debo Seck, 30 January 2023, https://africasacountry.com/2023/01/the-land-doesnt-lie.
35. Awa Thiam, *La parole aux négresses* [*Speak Out, Black Sisters*] (Paris: Denoël-Gonthier, 1978).
36. Later, the Cameroonian writer Calixthe Beyala, in response to 'Femme nue, femme noire', developed her theory of feminitude (a contraction of 'feminism' and 'negritude'). She has her character Irène quote the poem: '"Naked woman, Black woman, dressed in your colour, life, in your shape, beauty...". These lines are not part of my linguistic arsenal. You'll see: my words jolt and clank like chains. Words that clash, unhinge, unscrew, tumble, dissect and torture! Words that thrash, slap, break and crush! Anyone who feels uncomfortable should move on... Because here, there will be no lace bras, fishnet stockings, overpriced silk panties, rose or gardenia perfume, and even less of these ritualistic approaches to the femme fatale, borrowed from films or television.' Calixthe

Beyala, *Femme nue, femme noire* [*Naked Woman, Black Woman*] (Paris: Albin Michel, 2003), 11.

37. Gertrude Mutonkoley Mianda, 'Reading Awa Thiam's *La parole aux Négresses* through the Lens of Feminisms and Hegemony of English Language', *Atlantis: Critical Studies in Gender, Culture & Social Justice* 36(2) (2014), article 2.

38. Thiam, *La parole aux Négresses*, 20.

39. Echoing this, an article in *Fippu* on the struggles of Moroccan and Tunisian women is titled 'When the Pen Becomes a Weapon', *Fippu* 1 (August 1987): 28.

8

For Maria Mies

Silvia Federici

The death of Maria Mies, on the night of 14 May 2023, has been a great loss for the feminist movement, although as participants said at a memorial held on 4 June to celebrate her life, the powerful contribution that she has made to feminist theory and struggle ensures that she will continue to inspire us for a long time to come.[1] Maria Mies' work has been fundamental for the definition of a radical, anti-capitalist, anti-colonial feminist programme, a project that she has pursued throughout her life both with her writings, her teaching, and her incessant activism that was always the source of her theorising.

Born in Germany in a peasant family and raised in the post-World War II period, in a country that had to be reconstructed from the bottom up, Mies belonged to a generation of young people who saw the world changing in front of their eyes and could not ignore the political lessons of their time, which, after the defeat of Fascism, seemed to promise the beginning of a new world.

She also had a great capacity to learn from experience. She learned a lesson of courage from her mother who, in a country in ruin, did not give in to despair but set out to work to feed her family. As she wrote in her autobiography, *The Village and the World: My Life, Our Times* (2010): 'Our mothers were the "rubble women" who cleared the layers of debris and "enabled life to carry on".'[2] Mies never forgot this power of women to rise up when all seemed to be lost because they knew that the lives of other people depended on them and they could not afford to give in to pessimism. She also learned from her peasant father who, in ploughing the fields, hit the stones of a Roman road, teaching her that great empires too can fall.[3]

From her parents and from life in Auel, the village in the Eiffel where she spent her childhood, and where people lived communally from subsistence activities, she acquired the values that were to shape her politics: the love for the beauty, creativity and diversity of nature, the pleasure of cooperating with other people, and the value of a life based on the satisfaction of basic needs, rather than on unnecessary consumption.[4] But it was her decision in the 1960s to go, very young, as a teacher of German, to India, that changed her life.

The years that Mies spent in India were fundamental to her intellectual and political development. India opened the world to her. It was here, learning about the practice of Purdah from her female students, that (in her words) she first began to understand what patriarchy is as a social system.[5] In India, which was to become her second home, she not only saw the essential continuity between Nazism and colonialism, but began her life-long study of subsistence economies and women's work of reproduction, the subject of a research that she conducted on returning to the country in 1977.

By this time, both in Europe and the United States, a broad debate had developed among feminists on the role played by women's confinement to domestic work in the discrimination women have suffered in capitalism, as well as the reasons for the devaluation of this work and its function in the capitalist political economy. For some of us the key issue was to demonstrate that, despite its exclusion from economic categories, housework is a form of capitalist production, namely the production of labour power. But analysing housework from the viewpoint of her experience in India, Mies' focus was on its continuity with other forms of unwaged work, such as that

156

FOR MARIA MIES

performed within small peasant communities and by women in the Third World, and what it revealed concerning the logic of the capitalist system. One further lesson Mies drew from her experience in India was that, contrary to Marxist tenets, it is not always from the highest points of development that one can see the truth of the system. Not accidentally, back in Germany, the women with whom she most closely collaborated, Claudia von Werlhof and Veronika Bennholdt-Thomsen, all had a Third World experience.

With them, as well as with women in India and Bangladesh – like Vandana Shiva and Farida Akhter – as well as Renate Klein in Australia, Mies developed a powerful theoretical perspective, investigating the roots of discrimination against women, from hunting and gathering communities to capitalist societies, unmasking the myths that have served to justify it. Examining the reasons and the means by which male-dominated societies have systematically denied the productivity of women's lives and labour, and built the production of social wealth on conquest, colonisation and enslavement, has been one of the tasks of Mies' work. Thus, in her now classic *Patriarchy and Accumulation on a World Scale* (1985), she traced the historical development of patriarchal domination through different social/economic systems, always showing the essential continuity between the exploitation/devaluation of women, the exploitation of nature and the process of colonisation.

Indeed, before the rise of decolonial feminism, Mies saw how patriarchy and coloniality stem from the same predatory principle, that is driven to devalue what it most wishes and needs to appropriate. The title that she gave to her autobiography, the *Village and the World*, is reflective of this perspective, that never separated the local from the global, and always examined history, in particular that of capitalist development, from the viewpoint of the subjugated, the colonised, those whose life-production has sustained all economic activity though made invisible and unrecognised.

In her rewriting of history 'from below', the scope of her analysis has been consistently very wide, extending from a study of three-century long witch-hunts in Europe, to the role of slavery and colonisation in capitalist accumulation and the development of a sexual and international division of labour, to the place of women in national liberations struggles, from the Soviet Union to China and Vietnam. Although focusing primarily on the social/economic roots of social exploitation in all its forms, Mies has also not hesitated to confront onto-logical questions, proposing, for instance, that the historic anthropological differentiation between 'man-the hunter' and 'woman-the life-giver' may be traceable to the different ways in which men and women, by virtue of their constitutions, have related to the reproduction of life and the different tech-nologies they have produced in this process.

Such a thesis was no concession to a deterministic concep-tion of 'human nature'. While steering away from a concept of human nature as only a product of social manufacturing, Mies has rejected the idea that the experience of our bodies can ever be conceived as the encounter with a raw, animal-like purely biological reality, insisting that we always experi-ence our bodies in a culturally meaningful way, bringing our concerns and experiences to them and drawing practices and knowledges from them. The extent to which the fact that men's production of life (unlike women's) has required the use of tools has been responsible for men's specialisation in warlike practices – Mies' thesis concerning one of the origins of the sexual division of labour[6] – is debatable. It is worth men-tioning, however, as it demonstrates both her commitment to always go to the roots of social practices and understand in materialist ways the formation of social relations, and her belief that the attribution of meaning and value is an essential component of human life at all stages of its development.

From this viewpoint, she criticised Marx's and Engels' reductive conception of labour, which sees industrial work as the driving force of history, while assigning women's production of new life through procreation to the realm of biology and nature.[7] This biologistic bias – Mies argued – ignores that human beings are not enslaved by nature, but are able to 'appropriate' it and interpret it according to their needs and desires. As she put it:

> [Women] did not simply breed children like cows, but they appropriated their generative and productive forces, they analysed and reflected upon their own and former experience and passed it on to their daughters. This means they were not helpless victims of the generative forces of their bodies, but learned to influence them, including the number of children they wanted to have.[8]

According to this same principle, Mies also rejected the devaluation of the unschooled as people without knowledge and the devaluation of what is not industrially produced, from agricultural work to reproduction and care work, as something backward, ignorant and in need of being technologically reconstructed. Though influenced by Marxism, which she studied in the years of her activism in the student movement, she criticised Marx's admiration for industrial production, and in particular his belief that industrial development is a key factor in the construction of a communist society. Always ecologically minded, conscious of the devastating effects of industrialisation on the natural environment, she strongly warned that the Marxist vision of the extension of industrialisation to every part of the world would be utterly unsustainable and a historic catastrophe. Critical of Marx, she turned to Rosa Luxemburg, because of her understanding of the place of 'underdevelopment; in capital accumulation, and her belief that without 'colonies' capitalism cannot perpetuate itself.

'Colonies', however, in Mies, has a broader meaning than is generally intended. It signifies all the populations, social realities or territories that are appropriated, exploited, taken away from their ancestral inhabitants and in the process stripped of their history and devalued. In this sense, she has spoken of women as the 'last Colony'[9] precisely because in the capitalist sexual division of labour the contribution of their work to the production of life and reproduction of social relations has been made invisible, and harnessed in the service of men.

Mies famously labelled this process 'housewifisation', arguing that in time this was to become the model for all forms of work, as in the neoliberal economy all jobs would become precarious, underpaid, un-entitled to benefits, and in many cases invisible as work. In this respect as well, her theoretical perspective contrasted with Marx's, who projected that with capitalist development wage labour would be generalised, representing the paradigmatic work-relation in capitalism, and the terrain on which the struggle for human liberation would be combatted.

Like many feminists in the 1970s, Maria too believed that building a world in which the production of life is the goal and the centre of social organising must be the main objective of the feminist movement. This is a theme to which she returned over and over, starting with *The Subsistence Perspective* written in 1999 with Veronika Bennholdt-Thomsen.

A central concept in Mies' political vocabulary, 'subsistence' encompasses all that is valuable in our existence. It captures her vision of 'the good life', that is, of a future society, in which the production of life is no longer subordinated to the accumulation of wealth, and is accomplished instead in ways

FOR MARIA MIES

that neither destroy human beings nor the land. It also stands for a world of communal relations in which we recognise our essential interdependence and are responsible not only for our individual lives but for other peoples' lives and for the land.

Thus, since the early 1980s, Mies was a relentless critic of the capitalist drive to endless economic growth and of the renewed neoliberal globalisation of production. She saw that creating a major separation between production and consumption, and, for instance, importing food produced in the global south into Europe, not only destroyed the traditional agricultural cycles, but generated a culture of irresponsibility, in which it was increasingly difficult for people to understand where the food they ate came from, how it was produced, how the waste generated by consumption should be safely disposed of and so forth.

Mies understood that globalisation is a process of re-colonisation, leading to the expulsion of thousands from their ancestral lands, as fields, forests and crop-lands are privatised and devastated by various commercial ventures and extractivist technologies. As an alternative to this path, she advocated a relocalisation of agriculture and a move away from a model of consumption clearly bringing poverty and environmental destruction worldwide.

Critical of the technological destruction of nature, Mies was also one of the first feminists to speak against the new reproductive technologies, rejecting the ideology that portrays them as a means of women's liberation, presumably freeing women from the 'tyranny' of their biological make-up. Denouncing these technologies as turning the female body into a new field of investment and exploitation, and as having a eugenic intent, in *Ecofeminism* (1993), a book she co-edited with Vandana Shiva, she stressed the connection between the bio-engineering of the female body and the genetic engineering of plants and seeds, arguing that in both cases, under the guise of a rationalisation process, an industrial takeover of nature is at work, placing the process of reproduction of life under the control of science and the state.[10]

As typical of her methodology, she not only supported her arguments by pointing to the heavy medicalisation to which women's bodies are subjected by in vitro fertilisation, the passive, humiliating state to which they are reduced in this process, and the colonial relation inherent to surrogate mothering. Instead, she engaged in substantial historical research, reconstructing the history of the eugenic movement through the Nazi sterilisation campaigns, showing that bio-technology is driven by the same principle of selection and elimination, that it turns procreation into an industrial process, that it is already used (in India and China) to discard female foetuses, and ultimately that it aims 'to devalue children born of women as "inferior products"'.[11] In 'From the Individual to Dividual: The Supermarket of Reproductive Alternatives', she further warned against the institutional uses of the feminist affirmation of 'reproductive rights', and 'reproductive autonomy', to guarantee well-to-do women a child of their own through the exploitation of a class of 'breeder women',[12] at the very time that massive coercive sterilisation campaigns for population control were being conducted by the World Health Organization and other institutional agencies like the World Bank, denying populations of women in the 'Third World' the same right. Last but not least, she examined the ideology by which the new reproductive technologies have been promoted, tracing them back to their roots in the rationalist philosophies of the Enlightenment, pointing to their misogyny, their sexist biases and their tendency to place the foetus in a hostile position to the mother, and to drive mothering from the centre of the action, replaced by the doctor as the real life-giver.

As with her campaign against the global expansion of capitalist relations, in this case too, Mies did not only put forward

FOR MARIA MIES

her analysis and critique of reproductive technologies in her writing, but engaged in an incessant mobilisation against them, with feminists from different parts of the world organising conferences, workshops, protests – and writing manifestos, often in different languages. Thus, in the early 1980s, she was one of the promoters of *FINRRAGE*, a feminist network 'of resistance to reproductive and genetic engineering', whose very purpose was to campaign against this new colonisation of women's bodies. Among *FINRRAGE*'s main initiatives was the drafting of a resolution against genetic and reproductive engineering, which it then presented at the United Nations Nairobi conference in July 1985.

In the same years, Mies also began her life-long campaign against militarism and war, which had started in 1983 when she participated in the Hunsrück camp, set up by German feminists in front of two military bases where cruise missiles had been deployed. In this case as well she understood that warfare and militarisation could not prevail without the institutionalisation of patriarchal violence in everyday life, and that warfare is not only carried out with weaponry but is inherent to all economic policies, insofar as capitalism deprives millions of the resources needed to reproduce our lives. This was the message of a resolution Mies drafted in Leipzig in 1996, together with women from different NGOs, preparing strategies for the upcoming FAO Conference on Food Security, to be held in Rome later that year. At the same Leipzig conference, she also helped form Diverse Women for Diversity, a network and organisation that for years has highlighted the crucial role of women in food provisioning, and denounced the role of the International Monetary Fund (IMF), the World Bank and the World Trade Organization in spreading hunger across the world.

In 1998, with other women in Cologne, she launched a mobilisation against the Multilateral Agreement on Investment

(MAI), a policy that would have completely globalised the economy, disempowering all environmental and labour laws, giving all countries free access to any country's economy. This was the beginning of the first anti-globalisation movement in Germany,[13] sparked off by a conference held in Bonn that Mies helped organise, whose results she and Claudia von Werlhof later published in *Licence to Plunder* (1999).[14] A year later, Mies was in Seattle, a historic protest she spoke of as an inspiring example of 'globalisation from below' and a 'university of the streets'; in 2000, she joined the protest against the annual meeting of the IMF and the World Bank in Prague; in 2001, she was at the World Social Forum in Porto Alegre; in 2003, with other feminists in Cologne, she organised a conference on the occasion of the renegotiation of The General Agreement on Tariffs and Trade (GATT), which 'threatened to privatise government services, a move that would affect especially women'.[15] Meanwhile, after September 2001, her main concern became the relationship between globalisation and war, as she feared a new era had started, characterised by 'war without end' (the title of a book she published in German in 2004 – in which war would be described as 'destroying the very ability of societies to be *self-sufficient* and *self-reliant*').[16]

Mies' activism continued in her work as a university teacher, in Holland first and later in Germany. Through her courses and classroom discussions, she influenced a generation of feminists, several of whom, at a memorial held after her death, remembered, with love and gratitude, the inspiring and formative experience that her classes provided. All agreed that Mies thrived in collective work and possessed a unique ability to 'cut things to the essence' and identify the crucial issues, always striving to turn theory into action.

As with Marx, an early influence on her political formation, Mies believed that the point was not to interpret the world, but

FOR MARIA MIES

to change it, and, indeed, all her work had a practical translation identifiable in the activism that it inspired. Not only did she turn theory into practice, she theorised the need for practice. The principles she followed in this context were laid out in an important essay she wrote in the early years of the feminist movement, 'Towards a Methodology For Feminist Research',[17] where she presented a set of theses, defining a feminist viewpoint on the relation between knowledge and practice, in part motivated by the preoccupation that the developing Women Studies may become an academic affair. Acknowledging that Women's Studies was not invented by academic women but 'arose on the streets, in countless of women's groups ...', that is, that it was created by feminists who had a political goal, and that it would be used against women if it remained confined to academia, she insisted that feminist research and knowledge production should deliberately become part of the struggle against women's oppression, that it should be a process of collective 'conscientisation' and self-transformation, and provide a critique of all prevailing social scientific paradigms.

Mies' work has well exemplified these 'methodological guidelines for feminist research'. Indeed, few feminists have given us a broader and richer analysis of the motivations and consequences of capitalist development, in this process showing that feminism is not an appendage to existing social political perspectives, but a self-standing system, cutting across all disciplines, capable of providing a vision of the future speaking not only to women but also to the broader struggle for human liberation and the regeneration of nature. At a time when feminism was being appropriated by governments and the United Nations to integrate women as cheap labour in the global economy, and when many feminists embraced postmodern philosophies confining feminist critiques to textual analyses, Mies' work has been a powerful demonstration of the possibility of another, non-co-optable feminism, a subversive feminism, forged in the conviction that a radical change is needed in the material conditions of our lives, and this means a mobilisation to end the destructive power of patriarchal, capitalist, colonial relations.

Adding to her impressive theoretical work and her dedication to the struggle against capitalist patriarchy, Mies is also remembered and missed for her warmth, her vitality, the joy she brought to her work, and her political organising. Very creative, she made songs for every event, in one case, she even went to the podium, during a conference in Bonn, to sing it. She enjoyed her work and repeatedly reminded us that (contrary to common assumption, and even some of Marx's arguments) work can be a pleasure if it is not done under compulsion, under conditions of scarcity and for the accumulation of wealth. As she wrote in the introduction to *Ecofeminism* (with Vandana Shiva), in a world that seems bent on destroying all our means of our reproduction, our main task is to nourish the impulse, present in all living things, to reproduce themselves. Mies has done that in her relationships with the women with whom she has collaborated, in her relationships too with the many students that she has taught, and the thousands she has reached with her work, giving us not only a powerful analysis of the roots of social inequality and the road we need to take to create a more just world, but an example of transformative feminist practice, already bringing into existence, through day to day activism, something of the world to be created.

Mies was fond of remembering that, close to her death, rethinking her past, her mother exclaimed: "Wasn't that a good life!" We can now certainly affirm that of her life, as we mourn her loss, but celebrate the legacy that she has left us.

New York, July 2023

FOR MARIA MIES

Notes

1. The memorial was organised by Rene Gabri and Ayreen Anasta, with the participation of women from Maria's closest political family and her partner Sara Sarkar.

2. Maria Mies, *The Village and the World: My Life, Our Times* (North Geelong, VIC: Spinifex Press, 2010), xi.

3. All references to Mies' biography are taken from her book *The Village and the World*.

4. On the values that have inspired Maria's life, see her comments in the Epilogue to *The Village and the World*.

5. Ibid., 103.

6. See Maria Mies, *Patriarchy and Accumulation on a World Scale: Women in the International Division of Labor*, foreword by Silvia Federici (London: Bloomsbury Academic, 2014) (1st ed. London: Zed Books, 1986), Chapter 2, 'Social Origins of the Sexual Division of Labor', especially pp. 57–62.

7. Ibid., 45ff.

8. Ibid., 54.

9. Maria Mies, Veronika Bennholdt-Thomsen and Claudia Von Werlhof, *Women: The Last Colony* (London: Zed Books, 1988); and Veronika Bennholdt-Thomsen and Maria Mies. *The Subsistence Perspective: Beyond The Globalised Economy*, trans. by Patrick Camiller, Marie Mies and Gerd Wieh (London: Zed Books, 1999).

10. Maria Mies and Vandana Shiva, *Ecofeminism* (London: Zed Books, 1993), 187.

11. Ibid., 182–186 and 187.

12. Ibid., 198–217.

13. On Mies Anti MAI campaign, see *The Village and the World*, 263–268.

14. Maria Mies and Claudia Von Werlhof (eds), *Lizenz zum Plündern: Globalisierung der Konzernherrschaft – und was wir dagegen tun können* (Hamburg: EVA Europäische Verlagsanstalt, 1999).

15. See Mies, *The Village and the World*, 282–284.

16. Ibid., 285–286.

17. In Gloria Bowles and Renate D. Klein (eds), *Theories of Women's Studies* (London: Routledge and Kegan Paul, 1983), 117–139.

FEMINISM FOR THE WORLD

On these issues, see also Maria Mies, 'Feminist Research Science: Violence and Responsibility', in Maria Mies and Vandana Shiva, *Ecofeminism* (London: Zed Books, 1993), 36–54.

Selected Bibliography

Maria Mies, *The Lace Makers of Narsapur: Indian Housewives Producing for the World Market*. London: Zed Books, 1982.

Maria Mies, *Patriarchy and Accumulation on a World Scale: Women in the International Division of Labor*, Foreword by Silvia Federici. London: Bloomsbury Academic, 2014 (1st ed. London: Zed Books, 1986).

Maria Mies, Veronika Bennholdt-Thomsen and Claudia von Werlhof, *Women: The Last Colony*. London: Zed Books, 1988.

Maria Mies and Vandana Shiva, *Ecofeminism*. London: Zed Books, 1993.

Veronika Bennholdt-Thomsen and Maria Mies, *The Subsistence Perspective: Beyond The Globalised Economy*, trans. by Patrick Camiller, Marie Mies and Gerd Wieh. London: Zed Books, 1999.

Maria Mies, *The Village and the World: My Life, Our Times*. North Geelong, VIC: Spinifex Press, 2010.